The Hidden Mirror
The Truth About the Astral Clone

Allan Shepard
Booklas Publishing — 2025
Work originally written in 2023.

Original Title: *The Hidden Mirror*
Copyright © 2025, published by Luiz Antonio dos Santos ME.
This book is a non-fiction work that explores esoteric, spiritual, and psychoenergetic phenomena. Through an integrative and multidisciplinary lens, the author reveals the mechanisms behind the creation of astral doubles, their impact on the psyche, and practical strategies for spiritual protection, healing, and reintegration.

1st Edition
Production Team
Author: Allan Shepard
Editor: Luiz Santos
Cover Design: Studios Booklas / AstralLayer
Consultant: Dr. Malcolm Wyrd
Researchers: Jade Sommers / Felix Norwood / Anaïs Duval
Layout Design: Rowan Eckhart

Publication & Identification
The Hidden Mirror
Booklas, 2025
Categories: Esotericism / Spiritual Psychology
DDC: 133.9 – Parapsychology & occultism
CDU: 133.7 – Occult sciences

All rights reserved to:
Luiz Antonio dos Santos ME / Bookla
No part of this book may be reproduced, stored in a retrieval system, or transmitted by any means—electronic, mechanical, photocopying, recording, or otherwise—without prior and express permission from the copyright holder.

Summary

Prologue 10
Chapter 1 The Astral Clone 13
Chapter 2 Subtle Bodies... 20
Chapter 3 Spiritual Double 27
Chapter 4 Hermetic Wisdom.. 34
Chapter 5 Theosophical View.. 41
Chapter 6 Chaos Magic.. 48
Chapter 7 Shamanic Perspective.. 55
Chapter 8 Spiritist View... 62
Chapter 9 Thought-Forms.. 69
Chapter 10 Internal Causes 76
Chapter 11 External Causes 82
Chapter 12 Trauma and Fragmentation 89
Chapter 13 Negative Magic 95
Chapter 14 Energetic Bond 102
Chapter 15 Vital Drainage 109
Chapter 16 Mental Influence.. 115
Chapter 17 Astral Parasite.. 122
Chapter 18 Physical Signs.. 129
Chapter 19 Psychic Signs... 136
Chapter 20 Spiritual Detection... 143
Chapter 21 Initial Preparation 149
Chapter 22 Spiritual Cleansing 155
Chapter 23 Banishing Ritual 161

Chapter 24 Spiritual Protection 167
Chapter 25 Spiritual Help 173
Chapter 26 Shamanic Healing 180
Chapter 27 Magical Ritual 186
Chapter 28 Apometric Technique 192
Chapter 29 Internal Reintegration 198
Chapter 30 Final Care 204
Chapter 31 Complete Liberation 210
Epilogue 215

Sistematic Index

Chapter 1: The Astral Clone - Reveals the astral clone as an energetic duplicate coexisting on another plane, a psychic extension born from unintegrated aspects of the being.

Chapter 2: Subtle Bodies - Unveils the human energetic architecture through the subtle bodies, demonstrating how vibrational fissures can generate autonomous forms on the invisible plane.

Chapter 3: Spiritual Double - Investigates the archetype of the spiritual double across diverse cultures, presenting the astral clone as a particular and densified manifestation of this psychic duplication.

Chapter 4: Hermetic Wisdom - Interprets the phenomenon of the astral clone in light of universal Hermetic laws, revealing its mental and vibrational genesis and the keys to its transmutation.

Chapter 5: Theosophical View - Presents the Theosophical mapping of the subtle bodies, explaining how complex thought-forms condense in the astral ether, giving rise to energetic clones.

Chapter 6: Chaos Magic - Explores the intentional creation of astral servitors in Chaos Magic as a deliberate form of psychic duplication, addressing its potency and inherent risks.

Chapter 7: Shamanic Perspective - Offers the ancestral shamanic view of soul fragmentation and spiritual doubles, connecting them to the astral clone and practices of soul retrieval and healing.

Chapter 8: Spiritist View - Addresses the Spiritist perspective on the perispirit, its fragmentations, and manipulation by lower spiritual intelligences in the creation of subjugating fluidic clones.

Chapter 9: Thought-Forms - Details the creative power of mind and emotions in shaping thought-forms on the astral plane, explaining their evolution into complex entities like the astral clone.

Chapter 10: Internal Causes - Delves into the intimate origins of the astral clone, rooted in repressed emotions, unprocessed traumas, and psychic conflicts that generate energetic fragmentation.

Chapter 11: External Causes - Exposes how external consciousnesses, such as obsessors or negative magicians, can engineer astral clones through energetic manipulation for purposes of domination.

Chapter 12: Trauma and Fragmentation - Elucidates how deep trauma instigates soul fragmentation as self-protection, generating energetic duplicates that perpetuate the original pain on subtle planes.

Chapter 13: Negative Magic - Describes the ritualistic techniques of negative magic for the deliberate creation of astral clones, used as tools for psychic attack and spiritual sabotage.

Chapter 14: Energetic Bond - Reveals the nature of the vibrational cord that connects the astral clone to its creator, a dynamic channel of mutual influence and energetic sustenance.

Chapter 15: Vital Drainage - Analyzes how the astral clone acts in a parasitic mode, consuming the vital energy of its creator and generating physical, psychic, and spiritual exhaustion.

Chapter 16: Mental Influence - Details the insidious capacity of the astral clone to infiltrate the mental field, manipulating thoughts and emotions from within the psyche itself.

Chapter 17: Astral Parasite - Describes the clone's degeneration into an autonomous astral parasite, guided solely by the survival instinct through the host's energetic exploitation.

Chapter 18: Physical Signs - Points out the somatic reflections of the clone's presence, such as chronic fatigue, metabolic alterations, and weakened immunity, signs from the physical body to subtle interference.

Chapter 19: Psychic Signs - Delineates the psychic manifestations of the clone's influence, including mental confusion, intrusive thoughts, emotional instability, and a disturbing sense of internal otherness.

Chapter 20: Spiritual Detection - Presents the pathways for perceiving and identifying the astral clone, from subtle intuition to mediumistic faculties and specific energetic techniques.

Chapter 21: Initial Preparation - Guides on the indispensable internal preparation, strengthening the vibrational field and spiritual connection before confronting the clone's energetic structure.

Chapter 22: Spiritual Cleansing - Describes sacred practices of energetic cleansing (smudging, baths, crystals, prayers) to purify the aura and weaken the clone's vibrational foundations.

Chapter 23: Banishing Ritual - Explains the banishing ritual as an act of power and reaffirmation of spiritual sovereignty, aiming for the definitive cutting of ties with the astral clone.

Chapter 24: Spiritual Protection - Addresses the construction and maintenance of a protective vibrational shield after banishment, through spiritual discipline and mental and emotional vigilance.

Chapter 25: Spiritual Help - Discusses the importance of seeking qualified spiritual help in different lines of work to deal with complex interferences and promote deep healing.

Chapter 26: Shamanic Healing - Dives into shamanic practices of soul retrieval and extraction as ancestral pathways for reintegrating psychic fragments and dissolving dissociated energetic forms.

Chapter 27: Magical Ritual - Presents the magical ritual as a psycho-energetic operation aimed at confronting, deprogramming, and dissolving or reintegrating the astral clone through symbolic action.

Chapter 28: Apometric Technique - Details the spiritual technology of Apometry for precise diagnosis and treatment of astral clones, acting on multiple levels of the being through controlled unfolding.

Chapter 29: Internal Reintegration - Focuses on the crucial stage of welcoming and reabsorbing the legitimate parts of the psyche that were dissociated, filling the inner space with the authentic presence of the being.

Chapter 30: Final Care - Guides on the continuous care after liberation to stabilize the energy field, maintain vibrational coherence, and consolidate a new level of conscious living.

Chapter 31: Complete Liberation - Describes the state of complete freedom as the total restoration of the inner axis and spiritual sovereignty, where the soul commands its field without interference.

Prologue

There are moments when everything goes wrong. Paths once clear become murky, emotions tangle without explanation, and fatigue—physical, mental, and spiritual—settles in like a persistent fog. Many try to justify it: stress, bad luck, bad cycles. But what if the truth is deeper, older, more invisible?

What if what is operating against you isn't an external factor... but a hidden reflection vibrating in the shadows of your own energy field?

This book, now resting in your hands, is not a theoretical treatise. It is a map—detailed, revealing, and urgent—to understand the existence of a phenomenon as real as it is unknown: the astral clone. An energetic duplicate that, once formed, not only influences your life... it lives *through* it.

Yes, it might have been created by you, unintentionally, in moments of pain, anger, or trauma. But there is something even more unsettling: the astral clone can also be forged by someone who wishes you harm. A being of perverse intent, who molds your energy and transforms it into a copy of you, used as an instrument of spiritual sabotage.

Seems impossible? It is not.

For millennia, occult traditions and initiatory schools have recognized the existence of semi-autonomous astral fragments, created by another's will to spy, influence, sicken, or manipulate. And the cruelest part: when they are attacked, punished, or used, the impact reverberates directly onto you. Just like a voodoo doll connected to your essence, this duplicate suffers—and you suffer with it.

But then, why does no one talk about this?

Because the modern world has disconnected from the mysteries that sustain the true nature of being. We ignore the invisible. We laugh at the spiritual. And, in this skeptical laughter, we surrender our defenses to the very shadow we swore did not exist. Make no mistake: ignoring the astral clone does not make it disappear. It only makes it stronger.

This book brings a warning, but also a key. Here, you will discover:

How an astral clone is created—by you or by others;

How to identify it in your life through physical, mental, and spiritual signs;

How to dissolve this subtle presence before it consumes you.

You need to understand: if everything is going wrong, if patterns repeat, if you feel a strange presence within you, *something* is out of place. And, most likely, that "something" has your face.

This is not about superstition. It is about recognizing that you are a multidimensional being, with layers of existence that expand beyond the physical body. And in these layers, thoughts, emotions, and intentions crystallize. They take form. They act.

The astral clone is one of these fruits. It is born, it grows... and, if not understood, it imprisons.

But there is a way out. A journey of reconnection, purification, and reintegration. The knowledge contained in the following pages not only explains the phenomenon—it offers you real tools to face it. To regain control of your energy, your soul, and your existence.

Therefore, read carefully. Read with an awakened heart. Because perhaps—just perhaps—the key to freeing yourself from everything that has gone wrong in your life... lies here.

This is not just a book. It is a mirror. And the time has come to look at yourself without fear.

Luiz Santos Editor

Chapter 1
The Astral Clone

The existence of an energetic duplicate that coexists with the human being on another plane of reality is a phenomenon that transcends traditional conceptions of individuality. This duplication, although imperceptible to the physical senses, is intrinsically linked to the deepest constitution of the being, manifesting as an extension of the psyche on a non-material plane. The Astral Clone, as it is known in esoteric traditions, represents not just a metaphysical curiosity, but a reality with direct implications for the individual's emotional, energetic, and spiritual balance. It arises from the condensation of unintegrated internal aspects, reflecting, with varying intensity, traits, desires, fears, and psychic patterns of the originator. It is a living expression of fragments of the soul or mind that, for some reason, have escaped the unity of the conscious self and begun to act autonomously in a parallel vibrational field.

This type of duplication is not the result of science or genetic engineering, but rather of the energetic and spiritual dynamics involving every human being. Just as thought shapes realities on the subtle plane, intense and recurring emotions can, over time, give form to semi-material entities carrying the energetic signature of their generator. The astral clone is one such form: denser than a thought, yet subtler than physical matter. It can arise in moments of emotional imbalance, deep traumas, disordered spiritual practices, or even through external influence, when intentional forces act upon the individual's energy matrix. Its constitution, though subtle, is structured enough to allow interaction with the astral environment, other entities, and even the physical plane, through indirect influence on its creator.

The impact of an astral clone's existence is broad and multifaceted. By remaining linked to its originator through a permanent energetic connection, it directly influences the individual's mental, emotional, and spiritual states, often without them realizing the origin of the disturbances they face. This connection is like a bidirectional flow, where impressions and impulses constantly transit between the original and its duplicate. The intensity of this exchange depends on the creator's level of awareness of the phenomenon and the degree of autonomy the clone has developed. In more advanced cases, the clone can act with its own will, interfering in the individual's decisions and emotions, as if an unconscious reflection gained its own life. Identifying, understanding, and integrating it thus becomes an essential step on the path to self-knowledge and inner harmonization. It involves recognizing that the subtle world is not a fantasy, but a legitimate extension of reality, where forgotten fragments of ourselves await, silent, the chance to be heard.

Unlike the scientific clone, made from genetic material, shaped in laboratories, and laden with ethical and biological implications, the astral clone does not depend on cells, DNA, or incubators. Its substance is subtler, composed of astral or mental matter, and its origin occurs through means unknown to most. This being is sometimes not even perceived by its creator. It arises spontaneously, or, on some occasions, is forged by forces beyond human control. Its presence, however, is tangible in the effects it produces, reverberating sensations, thoughts, and emotional states that escape common logic.

The astral clone, once formed, maintains an invisible bond with its originator. This energetic link, often compared to the silver cord of astral projection, serves as a channel for communication and mutual influence. It is not a completely autonomous being, but neither is it totally submissive. It exists at an intermediate point between obedience and independence, an animated reflection of parts of the original's psyche, which, upon gaining form on the astral plane, begins to act on its own.

In mystical traditions, there are extensive descriptions of entities resembling the astral clone. Kabbalah, for example, speaks of the *dybbuk* – an entity that can possess or mimic a human soul. In Ancient Egypt, the *Ka* was a spiritual double that followed the individual during life and after death, with specific rituals for its nourishment and tranquility. In Vedic India, the concept of "Sharira" points to multiple bodies of the human being, one of which is the astral body, susceptible to unfolding and independent forms that can assume characteristics similar to those of the clone.

Although the notion of an "other self" might seem fanciful at first glance, human experience shows that there is more between heaven and earth than Cartesian systems of thought suppose. How many times has someone felt observed, only to turn around and find no one? How many people have narrated seeing themselves in dreams or visions, performing acts they never consciously undertook? These accounts, however diffuse they may seem, point to a persistent phenomenon in the collective psyche: the existence of another, mirrored in us, but acting under its own laws.

On the astral plane, where time and space are plastic and moldable by thought, the clone can assume multiple forms. In some cases, it appears identical to the physical body. In others, it may appear distorted, carrying in its appearance symbolisms of its creator's emotional states: shadows, scars, unusual colors. These signs are more than visual adornments – they are living records of the energy that generated it. An astral clone born of anger may seem threatening, while one originating from fear may be fragile, constantly trembling. But in all cases, it represents a real, albeit hidden, aspect of the being that gave rise to it.

There is a deep mystery surrounding how these clones are generated. Some esoteric lines state that every human being unconsciously creates astral forms based on their thoughts and emotions. The difference between these thought-forms and the astral clone lies in the degree of complexity and connection. The clone is not a mere floating idea: it is an animated fragment, a piece of the self endowed with movement and intention, even if rudimentary. In some situations, this entity is capable of interacting with others on the astral plane, establishing bonds, learning, and even, in extreme cases, acting against its creator's interests.

The danger of the astral clone lies precisely in this growing autonomy. When unidentified, it continues to absorb vital energy from the original, like a parasitic plant that, although seemingly harmless, gradually suffocates the tree hosting it. Sensations of inexplicable fatigue, sudden mood swings, vivid dreams with doubles, feelings of being "outside oneself," or even small memory lapses can be subtle signs of its presence. Often, the individual does not realize they are being influenced by a duplicate living in another dimension, but which, through the energetic link, sends constant impulses and interferences.

Beyond cases of spontaneous emergence, there are more serious situations where the astral clone is created by third parties. Obsessing spirits, negative magicians, or extraphysical entities can manipulate a person's subtle structure to extract a fragment of their energy and shape it into a duplicate. This copy is then programmed for specific objectives: astral espionage, psychic manipulation, energetic draining. In low-vibration magic rituals, this practice is known as parasitic duplication. The clone becomes a channel through which the manipulator accesses and influences the victim, without them perceiving the origin of the thoughts and emotions that come to dominate them.

The existence of the astral clone is not restricted to spiritually vulnerable or unbalanced individuals. Even people with great spiritual development can experience this phenomenon, especially when dealing with intense unresolved emotions. The difference lies in the capacity for identification and resolution. A conscious practitioner can perceive the duplicate and reintegrate it, dissolving the bond or healing the projected part of themselves. An unaware person, however, tends to suffer the consequences without understanding the causes, becoming hostage to a reflection that should be just a sign, and not a prison.

The bond between the clone and the original is one of the most fascinating and dangerous aspects of the phenomenon. It functions like an energetic artery, through which emotions, memories, and sensations flow. The clone, being a piece of the being, is naturally attuned to its frequencies. When the creator feels anger, the clone vibrates with anger. When they feel pain, the clone reverberates this pain. The problem is that this flow also occurs in reverse. If the clone is attacked on the astral plane, the original may feel physical or emotional pain. If the clone interacts with harmful entities, the host can be affected psychologically, without knowing where the disturbance comes from. This connecting cord is both a channel and a prison, requiring precise management so it doesn't become a path of self-destruction.

In some esoteric traditions, the astral clone is seen as an opportunity. It can be understood as an evolutionary mirror, a chance to confront denied parts of oneself. Instead of simply destroying it, some masters teach dialogue with the clone, understanding its motivations, and dissolving the energy animating it through integration. This, however, requires a high degree of self-knowledge and spiritual mastery, as the clone tends to resist reintegration, seeking to maintain its existence through energetic instinct. It is not uncommon for it to try to hide on the astral plane, disguise itself, or even lie to sensitive entities attempting to capture it. It wants to survive – and this will brings it dangerously close to a being with rudiments of consciousness.

Ultimately, the astral clone is a phenomenon that demands attentive observation, inner discipline, and profound respect for the reality of the subtle planes. Ignoring it will not make it disappear. On the contrary: by denying its existence, the person only yields more ground for it to act in their subtle field. Recognizing its presence is the first step to understanding what it represents: a displaced part of oneself, seeking meaning and survival. Whether as an unconscious reflection, malicious creation, or projected emotional fragment, the astral clone is always a warning that something is out of harmony. And where there is disharmony, there is also the possibility of healing – provided one has the courage to face their own shadow, even if it wears their face.

Chapter 2
Subtle Bodies

Understanding the human being requires diving beyond tangible matter, revealing a broader and more intricate constitution that transcends the limits of the physical body. True human nature expresses itself in multiple dimensions of existence, each governed by specific laws and vibrating at distinct frequencies, composing a multidimensional organism in constant interaction. It's not just about recognizing that there is more than meets the eye, but admitting that human experience is sustained by a complex energetic architecture. This architecture is formed by subtle bodies that coexist with the physical body and, although invisible, directly influence our emotional, mental, and spiritual states. This energetic reality is not metaphorical, but concrete in its own domain, structured in interdependent levels that, together, form what can be called the total identity of the being.

The subtle structure that surrounds and permeates the physical body is composed of interpenetrating layers, functioning as communication channels between the material world and the higher planes of consciousness. Each subtle body performs specific functions, responsible for capturing, processing, and distributing energies originating from the universe and the individual's own spiritual essence. This multiplicity has been recognized by different traditions throughout history, which, despite their cultural divergences, converged in the perception that the human being is much more than flesh and bone. From ancient Egypt to Vedic India, from Hermetic philosophy to contemporary spiritual doctrines, the idea emerges that individuality manifests in various vibrational layers, where each subtle body reflects a facet of the soul in its process of evolution and learning. These bodies, although distinct, are not isolated, but communicate and react in synchrony, like gears of the same cosmic mechanism.

A deep understanding of these subtle bodies not only illuminates the internal dynamics of the being but also offers keys to interpreting spiritual phenomena that, at first glance, might seem inexplicable. Imbalances in one of these levels, for example, are not restricted to the energetic field; they reverberate in emotions, thought, and even physical health. When there is harmony between the bodies, the being acts in fullness, guided by its higher center of consciousness. However, when there are cracks—caused by traumas, repressed emotions, or irresponsible spiritual practices—this cohesion breaks, and fragments of the psyche can detach, originating autonomous forms of existence on the subtle plane. It is at this point that space opens for the emergence of entities like the astral clone, whose understanding only becomes possible through recognizing the complexity of these invisible bodies. Thus, the study of subtle bodies presents itself not just as a metaphysical investigation, but as a vital necessity for anyone seeking to understand the hidden unfoldings of their own existence.

The concept of the astral clone cannot even be scratched without first understanding this multiplicity. The idea of subtle bodies is ancient, rescued from traditions that transcend religions and geographies. Egyptians, Hindus, Hebrews, Greeks, Tibetans, medieval alchemists, and modern mystics—all, in their respective languages, dealt with these invisible structures that, together, form the integral being. Each operates at a specific frequency and responds to its own laws, connecting the individual to different planes of reality.

The physical body is the densest and most limited. Subject to time, space, and gravity, it is also the most ephemeral. But enveloping it is what has been conventionally called the etheric double—an energetic replica of the biological body, whose primary functions include capturing and distributing vital energy, prana, chi. It is at this level that acupuncturists act when manipulating meridians, and it is here that the chakras are found, vortices of energy that regulate harmony between the physical and non-physical levels.

Above the etheric double vibrates the astral body. This is the true field of emotional experiences. Every emotion, before manifesting in bodily expressions or mental impulses, reverberates in this body. It is not just a storehouse of feelings, but also a vehicle for projection: it is with it that consciousness moves during lucid dreams, out-of-body experiences, astral travels. It is where encounters with spiritual entities occur and where reality assumes a plasticity moldable by will and belief.

Even higher is the mental body. Here reside thoughts, ideas, reasonings, but also obsessions, repetitive patterns, and mental constructs that can take on a life of their own. When a thought is charged with emotion and sustained long enough, it gains density in the mental body and begins to influence the other levels. From this point, the possibility of something more begins to delineate: a fragment, a copy, a double—the embryo of an astral clone.

In Spiritism, Allan Kardec synthesized these subtle bodies under the term "perispirit." For him, it is the link between the immortal spirit and the physical body, a semi-material envelope that captures the spirit's impulses and transmits them to the body, and vice versa. But the perispirit is not an indivisible unit: it is composed, in turn, of layers, and within them are contained both the astral and etheric bodies and other, even subtler levels. The perispirit is a living bridge, shaped by thoughts, emotions, and choices, and capable of faithfully reflecting a person's state of spirit.

These bodies normally operate integrated, united like the notes of a harmonic chord. The physical body feels the cold, the astral reacts with discomfort, the mental interprets and judges the sensation. Everything moves in unison, like a single, coherent organism. However, there are moments when this integration fails—due to trauma, spiritual practice, external manipulation, or emotional imbalance. And it is in this vacuum, in this moment of partial disintegration, that something can detach.

Spiritual unfolding, a phenomenon known by various names in different traditions, is the state where one of the subtle bodies temporarily moves away from the physical body, while still remaining connected to it by an energetic cord. During sleep, for example, the astral body partially frees itself and travels through the spiritual planes, sometimes without the individual having any conscious memory of it. But when this process becomes unstable—whether due to traumas, imbalances, or irresponsible practices—there is a risk that part of the astral body separates semi-autonomously. It does not return completely. It remains wandering. It becomes a duplicate. This fragment can continue absorbing vital energy, maintaining the connection with the physical body through a subtle cord. However, being detached from the central consciousness, it begins to react on its own, often reproducing old emotional patterns, repressed desires, unprocessed traumas. It ultimately becomes an astral clone.

The key is consciousness. As long as the being is awake and present in its multiple levels, its bodies align under the command of the Higher Self, forming a cohesive unit. But when there are cracks—and we all have them, to a greater or lesser degree—the energy field fragments, and the parts gain independence proportional to the degree of unconsciousness they are subject to. It is not possession, nor common obsession, but a kind of unconscious self-escape that materializes on another plane. It is not uncommon for emotionally unstable people, immersed in intense fears, angers, or desires, to inadvertently project parts of themselves out of the astral body, involuntarily creating these duplicates. The astral body, saturated by a single dominant vibration, tends to mold a fragment of that energy into a denser form. And in doing so, gives birth to an entity that, although originating from the being itself, no longer responds to its control.

This process is exacerbated by spiritual practices without preparation. People who venture into astral projection without adequate knowledge, who manipulate mental forces without self-awareness, or who make irresponsible use of entheogenic substances, can open doors within themselves that they do not know how to close. On these occasions, part of the astral or mental body detaches and cannot find its way back. Instead of dissolving into the ether, it fixes itself. It feeds. It molds itself. And, eventually, it lives—as a clone.

That is why understanding the subtle bodies is absolutely essential. Only through this understanding can one distinguish a common psychic disturbance from a complex energetic manifestation. The astral clone is not a symptom of madness, nor a mystical delirium. It is the result of a very real vibrational process, which obeys specific laws of the subtle world. Ignoring it is to allow it to strengthen. Understanding it is the first step to disarming it.

By recognizing oneself as a multidimensional being, endowed with bodies that go beyond the flesh, the individual begins to perceive that everything they feel, think, and do reverberates on different levels. There is no innocuous thought, nor isolated emotion. Everything leaves a trace. Everything is reflected in the subtle bodies. And every imbalance, every feeling nurtured long enough, can convert into form. Into life. Into another. Into a clone.

And what is outside—be it shadow or light—one day asks to return. Because every fragment wants to be whole. But while this reintegration does not occur, it will follow alongside, mirroring the essence of the being that created it, like an echo that does not fade.

Chapter 3
Spiritual Double

The coexistence of multiple expressions of the being on different levels of reality is one of the most intriguing manifestations of human nature. The presence of a spiritual double, although often relegated to the realm of legends and folklore, finds foundation in the subtle structures that compose the individual's psyche and energy body. This double is not a mere hallucination or a figment of fantasy: it is a real configuration, operating on a distinct vibrational plane, whose origin is deeply rooted in the unconscious and the spiritual layers surrounding the being. It represents the possibility of a parallel manifestation of identity, driven by impulses often unknown or unconscious, acting with a degree of autonomy in domains that escape ordinary perception. The notion that a human being can, even unintentionally, project a version of themselves that walks in another dimension emerges not as speculation, but as recognition of a phenomenon as old as spiritual thought itself.

This second "self," also called the spiritual double, is not necessarily configured as an adversary or a threat. In many traditions, it is perceived as a companion, an extension, or a form of consciousness unfolding. However, what defines its nature is not just its existence, but the emotional, mental, and spiritual state of the individual who originates it. When the being is in balance, the double acts as a useful reflection, an instrument for expanding perception, capable of performing tasks on subtle planes. But when there is imbalance, repression of emotions, unresolved traumas, or imprudent use of spiritual practices, this projection can acquire a dysfunctional form. At this stage, the double ceases to be a conscious resource and starts operating as an entity with its own will, generated by repressed contents that have escaped control. Its autonomy is not complete, but sufficient to interfere in the vibrational field and psychic processes of its creator.

The emergence of an astral clone is a specific and deepened example of this phenomenon. Unlike the traditional double, which tends to be transient and symbolic, the clone structures itself as a crystallized psychic fragment, animated by an intense emotional charge and sustained by energetic ties with the originator. It is, at the same time, product and reflection—a condensed manifestation of aspects of the self that found no expression on the conscious plane. Its prolonged existence requires a continuous flow of energy, leading it to maintain, often subtly and parasitically, its connection with the original matrix. Recognizing this presence, understanding its genesis, and integrating it into the field of consciousness is a task that demands not only spiritual knowledge but a deep dive into one's own inner abysses. Because this double, in its densest form, is the mirror not only of what we are, but of what we were unable to accept.

The term "doppelgänger," of German origin, is perhaps the best known in Western traditions. Literally, it means "double walker" or "one who walks alongside." In European folklore, this double was seen as a sinister omen. It was said that if someone encountered their own doppelgänger, it was a sign that death was near, or that great misfortune was approaching. The popular explanation was simple: the spiritual world had torn open and allowed the soul's shadow to manifest, warning that something had broken in the bond between body and spirit.

But the doppelgänger is not the only one. In Ancient Egypt, the "Ka" represented a kind of spiritual twin that accompanied the person throughout life. It was created at birth and continued to exist after death, needing spiritual nourishment through offerings and rituals. The Egyptians knew that the Ka could wander, visit the living, and even interact with the dreams of those left behind. It was a living spark of the individual's essence, almost like a parallel soul, connected by a sacred and unbreakable bond.

In Eastern traditions, such as Hinduism and Tantric Buddhism, there are references to the "illusory body" or "maya-kosha," a spiritual form reflecting the person's desires and karmas. In Tibetan Dzogchen practices, there are accounts of yogis capable of manifesting rainbow bodies or double forms to perform spiritual tasks on different planes simultaneously. They did not see this duality as evil, but as an advanced skill, a conquest of consciousness over matter.

In the shamanic traditions of North America, South America, and Siberia, we find accounts of "naguals," "spirit companions," or "shaman's doubles." These beings, which could take human or animal form, were sent on spiritual missions of healing, espionage, or battle. They were part of the shaman himself, an extension of his soul or consciousness, endowed with momentary autonomy. The existence of the double was considered sacred, and its management required great responsibility, under penalty of psychic fragmentation or loss of spiritual power.

Even in classic Western literature, the idea of the double appears recurrently. Goethe reported in his diary an encounter with his own doppelgänger during a moment of personal crisis. Dostoevsky wrote about the duality of the soul in his work "The Double," where the protagonist finds himself confronted by a bolder, crueler, and more unruly version of himself. Jung, in turn, developed the concept of the "Shadow"—a part of the psyche that is repressed and projected into the unconscious, potentially taking symbolic form in dreams, visions, or altered states.

It is in this vast ocean of symbols, accounts, and traditions that the astral clone inserts itself, as a specific manifestation of the spiritual double. The difference is subtle, but crucial. The double, in its classic versions, was generally a reflection, a symbolic image, or a temporary extension of consciousness. The astral clone, however, carries a more consistent intention of autonomy. It is not just a fleeting reflection, but an entity with some form of permanence and capacity for independent action, although linked by invisible threads to its originator.

The birth of an astral clone often occurs in moments of strong inner rupture. When a human being enters emotional or spiritual collapse, part of their psyche may detach in search of survival. It's as if the soul, unable to bear the weight of trauma, repression, or pain, projects a part of itself outward to avoid succumbing. This part then gains form on the astral plane. Initially, it may seem just a shadow, a repetition of gestures, a wandering energy. But over time—especially if it continues to receive energetic nourishment from the original—it gains form, will, and a kind of rudimentary consciousness.

In spiritual accounts of bilocation, for example, we see clear indications of this phenomenon. There are numerous documented cases of people seen in two places at the same time, with reliable witnesses guaranteeing they interacted with both versions. The Catholic Church recognizes this phenomenon in saints like Padre Pio and Saint Alphonsus Liguori, who, at various times, appeared simultaneously in different locations to perform healings, guidance, or spiritual tasks. These episodes are generally associated with the conscious unfolding of the astral body, but one cannot rule out the possibility that, in some cases, what manifested was a clone—a double created by necessity or by an intense will to help someone.

But spiritual duplication is not always benign. There are equally disturbing records of people who, while going through moments of extreme emotional tension, report having seen or felt the presence of an "other self," acting hostilely, threateningly, or manipulatively. This entity, in many cases, seems to feed on the original's emotional energy, amplifying negative feelings, generating mental confusion, recurring nightmares, and sensations of persecution. Such cases are not merely psychological. Many spiritualist traditions recognize that, once formed, the astral clone can become a parasite, acting as a "dark twin" that contaminates the person's emotional and spiritual life.

The bond between the clone and the original is deep and, at the same time, dangerous. It is not a bond of love, like between mother and child. It is more like a symbiosis—or, in more severe cases, vampirization. The clone needs the original to sustain itself. Without it, it disintegrates. But at the same time, it acts as if it were a separate being, claiming space, influencing thoughts, dreams, and behaviors. There are people who, unknowingly, spend years living under the influence of a double. They feel exhausted, emotionally uncontrolled, experience inexplicable internal conflicts, as if carrying two distinct wills within them. And, indeed, they are.

Recognizing this duality is a challenge. The astral clone does not present itself with a badge, nor does it knock on the door. It insinuates itself. It whispers. It manifests in the darkest corners of consciousness, where fear, anger, desire, and pain find residence. It may wear the face of the creator, but with a strange gleam in the eyes, as if something were out of place. It may appear in dreams, in mirrors, in moments of spiritual fragility. And it always leaves a mark: the feeling that something within oneself is not in harmony, that there is an invisible presence that is not entirely you.

The spiritual double, in its archetypal forms, has been seen for millennia as a warning, an intermediary, a reflection. The astral clone is its modern and complex unfolding—a reflection that gained will, a warning that never ceased to echo, an intermediary that decided to walk on its own. It is proof that we are not indivisible. We are made of layers, of voices, of fragments. And sometimes, one of these fragments decides to walk alone. In this invisible world where everything vibrates and connects, the existence of an astral clone is not only possible—it is a natural consequence of who we are and how we live. It is the living mirror of our choices, traumas, and potentials. And like any mirror, it can reflect both light and shadow. Understanding it is finally understanding that the greatest mystery lies within ourselves—and that perhaps we have never walked alone.

Chapter 4
Hermetic Wisdom

The ancestral wisdom of Hermeticism offers a solid and profoundly revealing foundation for understanding the subtle manifestations of existence, such as the phenomenon of the astral clone. Far from being a reverie or mystical accident, this energetic duplication finds logical support in the universal laws governing all planes of reality. By delving into Hermetic teachings, a worldview unfolds in which everything that exists, from the densest to the most ethereal, obeys fundamental immutable principles. These principles not only explain the structure of the universe but also guide the conduct of the seeker who wishes to become a co-author of their reality. In this context, the astral clone emerges not as an anomaly, but as a natural consequence of internal imbalances projected onto the subtle plane—a predictable effect of vibrational causes sustained over time.

The Hermetic tradition is not limited to transmitting theoretical knowledge; it proposes a path of self-mastery, where the awakened being learns to observe, understand, and transform the forces acting within them. By recognizing that all is mind, as taught by the Principle of Mentalism, one understands that reality is molded from thought. And when thoughts align with intense and recurring emotions, they form energetic molds capable of giving rise to autonomous entities on the astral plane. The clone, in this sense, is a legitimate product of the creative mind, a living externalization of unintegrated psychic contents.

Considering the principles of Correspondence and Vibration, it becomes evident that what repeats internally—such as emotional patterns, unresolved traumas, or repressed desires—will find resonance in other layers of the being. The clone is this condensed echo, a replica vibrating at the same frequency as the emotional origin that generated it. By delving into polarity, rhythm, and causality, Hermeticism reveals that everything in creation has its complementary opposite, that nothing remains immutable, and that every effect derives from a specific cause. Understanding these laws allows the individual not only to identify the origin of the astral clone but also to develop the means to dissolve or reintegrate it. The clone ceases to be seen as an external threat and comes to be recognized as part of one's own energy field, a manifestation carrying a coded message about the creator's inner state.

Hermeticism, therefore, does not offer a perspective of fear, but of lucidity. It teaches that every thought is a magical act, every emotion is a creative vibration, and that every human being possesses, within themselves, the power to transform the forms they generate. Thus, the astral clone is unveiled as a hidden master, pointing to the neglected aspects of the self and inviting the inner work of transmutation and integration.

Hermeticism, attributed to Hermes Trismegistus—a mythological figure synthesizing the Egyptian god Thoth and the Greek Hermes—maintains that the universe is governed by seven immutable principles. These principles are not doctrines to be believed, but operational keys describing the structure of subtle and material reality. The scholar who understands them not only observes the world but shapes it. And it is precisely at this point that the astral clone ceases to be an obscure mystery and becomes a predictable energetic equation.

The first Hermetic principle, that of Mentalism, declares: "The All is Mind; the universe is mental." This implies that everything that exists is, ultimately, a product of the divine mind. And since the human being is made in the image and likeness of the All, they too create realities with their mind. Thoughts, emotions, mental images, and beliefs are not just abstractions; they are seeds. And when these seeds are watered with sufficient energy and attention, they germinate on the astral plane. Thus, the genesis of the astral clone can be seen as the materialization of a recurring idea or emotion that, by mental force, assumes form and autonomy.

The second principle, Correspondence, echoes the famous axiom: "As above, so below; as within, so without." The astral clone is a mirror. It is the reflection of a part of the being in another dimension. It is a duplication respecting the Law of Correspondence: if there is a persistent pattern within the being, it will express itself at some external point, whether on the physical, emotional, or astral plane. Unresolved resentment, for example, may remain latent in the mind, but it can also manifest as a living reflection on the subtle plane—a clone driven by rancor, wandering and seeking revenge on behalf of the creator who may no longer remember the original grievance.

Another principle illuminating the phenomenon is Vibration: "Nothing rests; everything moves; everything vibrates." Every thought, every emotion, every intention possesses a specific frequency. When a vibrational pattern becomes dominant in a person's energy field, it tends to condense. Like in an electrical storm, emotional clouds accumulate to the point of discharge: the lightning strikes, or in this case, the astral clone appears. It is the precipitation of a constant vibration, materialized on the subtle plane by energetic affinity. And once formed, it will continue vibrating at the same frequency that originated it, feeding back into the cycle.

The Principle of Polarity teaches that "everything is dual; everything has poles; everything has its pair of opposites." The astral clone is, from this perspective, the complementary pole of awakened consciousness. It embodies what has been rejected, repressed, or neglected. If a person lives only their luminous persona, the clone may represent the shadow—the dark, unintegrated side seeking existence by its own means. However, this does not make it inherently evil. It is merely the other side of the coin. The danger lies in the lack of balance between the poles, in ignorance of its existence, and in the refusal to face what it represents.

The principle of Rhythm reveals that "everything flows, out and in; everything has its tides; all things rise and fall." This shows us that nothing remains static. Not even the clone. Its power and influence fluctuate according to the creator's inner cycles. When the originator is strengthened, centered, harmonized, the clone weakens. When the individual plunges into emotional instability, obsessive thinking, or unconscious spiritual practices, the clone gains strength. Like an astral tide, it advances and retreats, seeking opportunities to manifest more intensely.

The sixth principle, Cause and Effect, is perhaps the most revealing: "Every cause has its effect; every effect has its cause." The astral clone does not arise by chance. It is the effect of a specific cause: a reiterated energetic pattern, an intense and unexpressed will, an undigested trauma, a poorly conducted magical practice. It is a direct consequence of a series of choices and internal states. By understanding it as an effect, it becomes possible to trace its origin and, consequently, transform it. The true magician, Hermeticism teaches, does not lament effects—they modify causes.

The principle of Gender states: "Gender is in everything; everything has its masculine and feminine principles." This principle refers to the creative duality of the universe: the masculine as emitting force, the feminine as receptive force. The creation of an astral clone requires the presence of these two polarities. Thought (masculine) sends the seed, emotion (feminine) receives and nurtures it. When these two energies unite with sufficient intensity, they produce a form: an entity on the subtle plane. Therefore, both mind and heart are involved in this process of energetic duplication. It is not enough to think—one must feel. And it is not enough to feel—one must think repeatedly. The astral clone is, therefore, the legitimate child of the marriage between thought and emotion.

But Hermeticism not only explains the genesis of the astral clone; it also offers paths for its dissolution. The Law of Transmutation, implicit in the seven principles, teaches that everything can be changed from one form to another—provided its nature is understood. Thus, a clone born of anger can be transmuted by compassion; a duplicate generated by fear can be reintegrated through self-knowledge. The Hermetic occultist does not blindly destroy what they created. They transmute. They reintegrate. They understand that everything is part of the One, and that even what frightens carries the divine spark within it.

It is important to remember that ancient Hermeticists did not view the subtle planes as metaphors. For them, the astral plane was as real as the physical, albeit governed by different laws. They understood that every magical act, every prayer, every mental visualization, every intense emotion was an act of creation on this plane. They knew they could, intentionally or not, generate forms and entities—and therefore recommended constant vigilance over their own thoughts and desires.

Hermes Trismegistus, in his writings, made it clear: "He who knows himself knows the universe." This maxim is the core of Hermetic wisdom. And applying it to the issue of the astral clone reveals the path to the solution: self-knowledge. By discovering one's own polarities, investigating the hidden causes of thoughts and emotions, taking responsibility for the creations emanating from oneself, the individual can not only dissolve astral clones but prevent new ones from arising.

There is no place for spiritual victimhood in Hermeticism. Everything that exists in a person's life has been attracted, permitted, or created by them. The astral clone is, therefore, an invitation: to revisit repeating thoughts, persistent feelings, secret desires never faced. It is the subtle embodiment of what was rejected. And as long as it is ignored, it will continue knocking at the door of consciousness, demanding to be seen.

Hermetic wisdom does not offer ready answers—it offers keys. Keys to open the portals of perception, responsibility, transformation. And once one understands that everything in the universe is mental, one also understands that every clone can be undone with the same power with which it was created: the power of the awakened mind, allied with conscious will and a heart aligned with the All. Thus, the clone ceases to be a hidden enemy and becomes a temporary master, whose mission is to point to what within us needs to be transmuted. And when this lesson is understood, the duplicate dissolves—not in battle, but in light.

Chapter 5
Theosophical View

The Theosophical approach to the multiple bodies of the human being establishes a detailed map of the individual's hidden constitution, in which each vibrational layer fulfills a specific function in the evolutionary process of consciousness. Inserted in this context, the phenomenon of the astral clone ceases to be an isolated mystery or a mystical event of random nature and occupies an intelligible place within the dynamics between the subtle bodies and the astral plane. Theosophy, by articulating Eastern and Western knowledge with philosophical and spiritual rigor, reveals that everything in the human being is energy in motion, shaped by persistent mental and emotional patterns. Thus, the astral clone emerges as a legitimate—though dysfunctional—expression of a dissociated part of the psyche, condensed into vibrational form in the astral ether, which is the quintessential plastic field for mental and emotional creations.

The Theosophical distinction between the physical, etheric, astral, lower and higher mental bodies, and the higher spiritual levels allows for understanding the complexity of the forms inhabiting the invisible plane. The astral clone, within this scope, is an entity formed from the overload of one or more of these layers, especially the astral body or the lower mental body. It is not an external entity, but a portion of the individual themselves that, due to traumas, intense desires, or maladjusted esoteric practices, separates from the central consciousness and acquires a certain degree of autonomy. This separation occurs gradually: it begins with a recurring thought or emotion, which, by fixing itself over time, attracts subtle matter and organizes itself as a living form on the astral plane. The energy sustaining it does not come from outside, but from the creator themselves, who, even unconsciously, continues feeding this fragment with their attention and vibration.

Theosophy teaches that the universe is constituted by rigorous laws, among them the Law of Vibrational Attraction, according to which like attracts like. This principle explains not only the formation of the astral clone but also its capacity to associate with external forces, such as astral larvae, collective thought-forms, or artificial elementals. A clone generated by fear, for example, vibrates at the frequency of fear and attracts entities from the lower astral that feed on this energy. The result is a parasitic symbiosis, which intensifies the deleterious effects of the clone, making it not just a reflection of the creator, but also a channel for forces aiming to further unbalance their energy field.

Theosophy, however, does not present this scenario as a sentence, but as a warning sign—an opportunity for rebalancing through self-knowledge, emotional purification, and the conscious use of will.

Each astral clone, no matter how dense or disturbing it may seem, is a reminder that the human being is a creator on all planes, and that their own light is capable of dissolving even the most resistant shadows.

Helena Petrovna Blavatsky, the founder of the modern Theosophical movement, spoke insistently about the "linga sharîra," a Sanskrit term referring to the lower subtle body—an energetic replica of the physical body, sensitive to the individual's emotions and thoughts. Blavatsky identified it as the "astral double," an intermediate layer serving as the mold and support of incarnate life. According to her, this body was susceptible to ruptures, unfoldings, and influences. It was not just a passive vehicle, but a moldable entity, capable of interacting with the spiritual plane and, under certain circumstances, behaving like a semi-autonomous being. It is at this point that the Theosophical conception aligns with the notion of the astral clone. When the linga sharîra detaches unstably or remains on the astral plane after intense experiences—such as traumas, states of trance, or poorly directed spiritual practices—it can crystallize a part of the individual's essence. This crystallization, fed by emotional and mental residues, begins to act as an animated reflection: the clone.

The difference between this phenomenon and a mere thought-form lies in the vibrational density and internal complexity of the created entity. An astral clone, according to the Theosophical perspective, is not just an externalized thought, but a vitalized fragment of the being itself, with memory, emotion, and, sometimes, rudiments of consciousness.

Annie Besant and Charles Leadbeater, continuators of Blavatsky's work, refined the understanding of the subtle bodies. For them, the astral body was the vehicle of emotions, while the lower mental body processed concrete thoughts and the higher mental body connected to abstract mind and higher intuitions. This distinction made it possible to precisely map the different forms of energetic duplication. For example: a clone generated by an intense emotion, like hatred or fear, would tend to form in the astral body; whereas a clone formed by obsession or continuous desire could emerge from the lower mental body. In both cases, the risk was the same: creating a being that not only moved away from the central consciousness but began to actively influence it.

In the Theosophical view, the universe is permeated by a plastic substance called "astral ether," which serves as the basis for the manifestation of forms and thoughts. It is in this ether that mental and emotional creations condense. When an emotion is nurtured constantly and allies with a powerful mental image, it crystallizes in this field, acquiring form, movement, and even a certain durability. The thought-forms thus generated can be simple—like arrows of anger or spheres of affection—or complex, like true entities. Theosophists describe these beings as "astral shells," "artificial elementals," or even "egregores," depending on the origin and nature of the impulse that generated them. It is precisely in this gradation that the astral clone is found. It is a complex thought-form, but with a peculiarity: it is born not just from a specific desire or emotion, but from an entire portion of the psyche projected onto the subtle plane. It's as if a part of the being, charged with intention, memory, and emotional pattern, detached from the whole and acquired its own existence. This explains why the clone often presents the same features, voice, and mannerisms as the creator—it is, in fact, a partial copy, animated by the forces that gave rise to it.

Furthermore, Theosophy recognizes the existence of entities called "astral larvae"—degenerate forms that cling to human emotions to feed. Although not clones proper, these larvae can parasitize the clone, strengthening it and making it more hostile or resistant to dissolution. This occurs because the clone, being a vibrational entity, is vulnerable to symbiosis with other beings of the lower astral. Such coupling makes it even more dangerous, as it begins to act not only as a reflection of the creator but also as an instrument of external forces exploiting the opened energetic breach.

The Theosophical view also warns about the dangers of working with esoteric practices without inner preparation. The improper use of mantras, visualizations, evocations, or projections can inadvertently generate energetic duplicates. In many cases, the poorly guided spiritual student creates a reflection of themselves on the subtle planes that, instead of helping growth, begins to interfere in daily life with emotional disturbances, mental blocks, and spiritual confusion. The person feels divided, exhausted, as if constantly drained by something invisible. And they are—by themselves, in duplicate form.

There is also, in Theosophy, the concept of "mental elementals"—forms generated by the collective mind of humanity. When a pattern is shared by many people—such as fear, guilt, desire for power—these emotions gain their own life on the astral plane, becoming semi-intelligent entities. In extreme cases, these collective forces can merge with an individual astral clone, forming a highly influential hybrid. The result is a being with personal motivation (from the creator) and collective strength (from the associated egregore), capable of acting with great power in the spiritual field.

However, Theosophy does not limit itself to describing the problem. It points to paths of solution. To dissolve an astral clone, one must act on three levels: first, cease the flow of energy feeding it, interrupting thoughts and emotions associated with it; second, raise the overall vibration of the energy field, through practices of purification, study, prayer, and altruistic service; and third, reintegrate the dissociated part, through self-knowledge and transmutation of the causes that originated the unfolding. This triad—interruption, elevation, and reintegration—is the core of Theosophical healing.

The role of will is also central. Theosophists teach that will is the soul's most powerful tool. When directed with clarity and compassion, it is capable of reabsorbing any projected form, no matter how complex. Therefore, it is not enough to wish for the end of the astral clone—one must understand it, accept it as part of the evolutionary process, and then, with firmness and love, command its dissolution or reintegration.

Another important aspect is the role of the Masters of Wisdom. In Theosophy, it is believed that spiritually advanced beings—the Mahatmas—accompany and instruct sincere disciples. Often, the dissolution of an astral clone is only possible with the assistance of these mentors, who operate on higher planes and help recalibrate the disciple's energy field. Sincere prayer, continuous study, and selfless service are ways to connect with these intelligences and receive their silent, yet powerful, aid.

Thus, the astral clone, in the Theosophical view, ceases to be an obscure accident and becomes a milestone in the evolutionary journey. It signals that fragmentation occurred, but also offers the chance for healing. It is shadow, yes, but also an invitation to light. Its existence is a reminder that we are co-creators on all planes, and that even our mistakes can become portals of wisdom—if we look at them with courage and know, finally, how to walk towards integration.

Chapter 6
Chaos Magic

Chaos Magic presents itself as an operative field where the magician's creative freedom overrides dogmas, traditions, or inherited limitations. With a pragmatic and deconstructed approach, it establishes a flexible structure where personal power is the main lever for transforming reality. Instead of depending on fixed symbolic systems, the practice develops through direct experimentation, ritualistic adaptation, and intentional manipulation of symbols, emotions, and archetypes. Within this context, the magician assumes the role of architect of their own mystical experience, redesigning their beliefs according to the demands of each magical operation. The absence of a closed doctrine gives Chaos Magic a unique vitality: in it, there is no separation between the subject and the object of magic—both merge into a dynamic field of possibilities where will manifests plastically and responsively.

The deliberate creation of entities on the astral plane, such as the so-called servitors, arises from the premise that everything is moldable as long as it is charged with intention and energy. The process involves the conscious externalization of fragments of the individual psyche, which, when organized through symbols, names, forms, and purposes, begin to act as semi-autonomous agents in the subtle field. This practice, profoundly introspective and highly personalized, leads the operator to confront latent aspects of themselves while projecting these portions outward in symbolic form. This externalization, however, does not occur randomly: it requires mental focus, emotional clarity, and symbolic mastery, as any instability in intention can result in unbalanced or uncontrolled constructs. Thus, the magician needs to develop refined sensitivity to recognize the extent to which they are operating with control and when they begin to be operated by what they created.

By allowing the conscious manipulation of astral entities, Chaos Magic opens up a universe of action where the astral clone ceases to be an accidental or unconscious manifestation and assumes the status of a strategic tool. This transition from the unconscious to the deliberate redefines the practitioner's role: they are no longer a passive subject of spontaneous psychic experiences, but an engineer of the invisible. Through techniques such as the use of sigils, ritualistic gestures, visualizations, and directed meditations, the operator constructs, activates, and sustains these fragments with defined objectives—whether for protection, interdimensional communication, or consciousness expansion. Responsibility, therefore, becomes proportional to the degree of freedom offered by this form of magic. Creating astral clones or servitors is not just an act of energetic projection, but a deep foray into the cartography of the soul, where the magician must constantly recognize themselves in their creations to avoid getting lost in them.

Unlike the spontaneous manifestations described in older traditions, Chaos Magic proposes the intentional generation of energetic duplicates. The practitioner shapes, with symbolic and emotional precision, a portion of their own psyche, imprints a purpose on it, and launches it onto the astral plane as an active entity. This entity, called a servitor, can be programmed for specific tasks: protection, attracting opportunities, spiritual espionage, or even sabotaging hidden enemies. The servitor is, by definition, a fragment of the magician's consciousness, animated by will and fed by vital energy. It is, therefore, a type of astral clone, created with method and intention.

Phil Hine, one of the main popularizers of contemporary Chaos Magic, describes this process with almost scientific clarity. According to him, every servitor is a symbolic representation of a need or function. The magician, by creating a symbol, name, and identity for this fragment, gives it psychic existence on the subtle plane. Then, through personalized rituals—which may involve meditation, visualization, gestures, sigils, and mantras—the practitioner infuses energy into the construct, activating it as a semi-autonomous entity. This creation begins to inhabit the operator's astral field, but with a certain freedom of action, as long as it obeys the originally programmed guidelines.

The parallel with the astral clone is inevitable. Both are energetic duplicates of parts of the original psyche. The difference lies in the degree of consciousness of the process. While the astral clone often arises unconsciously, resulting from traumas or dense emotional patterns that escape rational control, the servitor of Chaos Magic is created with full knowledge and intention. However, this does not make it risk-free. Many practitioners report that their servitors, once created, began acting beyond their designated functions, developing their own patterns, becoming obsessive, aggressive, or simply too autonomous. In other cases, old servitors refused to be undone after completing their tasks, requiring specific closing ceremonies or being "forcibly absorbed" back into the magician's energy field.

This leads us to a crucial point: every psychic creation, when fed with intensity, tends to develop an impulse for self-preservation. The astral clone, born of fear or pain, seeks to continue existing. The servitor, molded to act as a tool, may end up believing its existence is necessary. The boundary between servitor and astral clone thus becomes thin. It only takes the operator losing control over their creation, stopping conscious feeding but still maintaining emotional or mental links with it, for the servitor to escape their domain and convert into a clone—a reflection of them, now untamed.

There are documented cases in contemporary occult groups where servitors created for personal protection began manifesting hostilely towards any form of criticism, attracting discord, ruptures, and negative events. Upon investigating these occurrences, it was realized that the servitors had absorbed repressed traits of arrogance, insecurity, or anger from the creator themselves. Like good clones, they not only executed orders but also amplified what was latent in the originator's psyche. The creation, as always, reflected the creator—including in their most unconscious aspects.

This phenomenon reinforces the fundamental principle of Chaos Magic: the universe is moldable by consciousness, but it must be observed responsibly. By manipulating symbols, archetypes, and fragments of their own soul, the magician is playing with subtle fire. They can create wonders, but also monsters. And many of the monsters haunting modern operators are not external—they are their own astral reflections, energized and released in the name of personal power.

There is a particularly revealing technique within Chaos Magic called *splitting*, which consists of consciously separating a part of the psyche—such as a specific emotion, a skill, an inner archetype—and externalizing it in the form of an entity. By naming it, drawing it, visualizing it, and assigning commands to it, the practitioner transforms it into an externalized agent. It is at this point that the astral clone ceases to be a mere consequence and becomes a resource—dangerous, but powerful. A skilled operator can use the clone as an explorer of the astral plane, as a psychic defense against attacks, or even as a double in bilocation practices.

But there is a price. Every created clone requires maintenance. It needs energy, focus, and delimitation. If these conditions are not maintained, it becomes unstable. It may start acting impulsively, feeding directly from the creator's energy field, like a sophisticated parasite. It can interfere with dreams, relationships, health. It can, ultimately, want to take the original's place—not out of malice, but pure energetic logic: vital space must be filled, and if the originator is fragmented or weakened, the clone takes command.

The dissolution of an astral clone generated via Chaos Magic follows principles similar to its creation. The operator must first revoke its programming, thank it for the function performed (if applicable), and perform a ritual of reabsorption or symbolic burning. This may involve destroying symbols, sigils, or representations of the clone, with the clear intention of dismantling and transmuting it. Some schools recommend using purple candles (color of transmutation), specific crystals (like amethyst or obsidian), and salt baths to definitively break the energetic bond.

Another path is compassionate reintegration. Instead of destroying the clone, the magician can call it back, visualizing it as a wounded or dissociated aspect of themselves. They welcome it, forgive it, integrate it. In this process, symbolic visions, intense emotional discharges, and changes in the operator's mental pattern often occur. It is an advanced form of magical self-therapy, where the clone ceases to be a separate entity and returns to its original source.

Ultimately, Chaos Magic offers us not only tools to understand the astral clone but also instruments to create, control, and dissolve it. It does not moralize the process—it only describes and operates it. But its radical freedom demands radical responsibility. Creating a clone can be an act of power, but also an invitation to ruin if done without self-knowledge. Every operator must remember: what you create in the astral, also creates in you. The astral clone is a mirror, a response, a warning. It is, in essence, a form of your own consciousness crying out for integration. And if chaos is the origin of all creation, let it also be the fertile ground for reconciliation between what you are and what you project. Because in the end, every magician is also their own apprentice—and every clone, their most sincere reflection.

Chapter 7
Shamanic Perspective

The shamanic worldview recognizes the existence of multiple simultaneous planes where the human being manifests not as an indivisible entity, but as a dynamic set of interconnected parts that can shift, sicken, or get lost. In this holistic and ancestral understanding of reality, body, mind, spirit, and emotions form an energetic network that interacts with the invisible world, natural cycles, and spirits. Shamanic practice, founded on millennia of observation and direct experience with the spiritual world, treats these internal dissociations as real and concrete events, demanding healing, reintegration, and reconnection. It's not just about metaphors or symbols, but palpable manifestations in the individual's energetic and spiritual field. It is through this living and deeply experiential perspective that the phenomenon of the astral clone inserts itself as an expression of the fragmented soul—a reality that shamans recognize, confront, and transform.

Throughout their visionary journeys, facilitated by chants, drum beats, sacred plants, and expanded states of consciousness, the shaman acts as a mediator between worlds. They detect energetic imbalances not only in the physical body but also in the subtle fields where emotional memories, ancestral patterns, and lost soul fragments reside. The understanding that traumas, shocks, or intense spiritual experiences can cause parts of the soul to detach is central to this system. And these fragments, far from being just inert energies, carry traits of the individual's consciousness: emotions, desires, fears, intentions. When not retrieved, these pieces of the being can crystallize into semi-autonomous forms in the spiritual worlds, becoming true living echoes of the original trauma. These forms, operating in parallel to the incarnated being, are identifiable as spiritual duplicates—and it is precisely at this point that the concept of the astral clone resonates with shamanic knowledge.

Ancestral wisdom does not consider these duplicates aberrations or errors, but legitimate expressions of a spiritual self-protection process that, when prolonged, becomes dysfunctional. Thus, the astral clone is understood as a symptom of fragmentation and, at the same time, a map for healing. It points to the place of loss, of rupture. Shamanic work, then, seeks not only to eliminate this reflection but to reintegrate it into the totality of the being. It is an approach of welcoming, listening, and reconnecting with the lost essence. The practice of soul retrieval, essential in this process, symbolizes a return to wholeness, where each part of the being finds its place in the whole. From this viewpoint, the astral clone is more than an energetic phenomenon—it is a call from the soul for the human being to return to themselves, healed, complete, and in communion with the whole.

Shamanic spirituality does not recognize rigid boundaries between body, mind, and spirit. Everything is energy in flow. And all energy can shift. When an individual suffers an emotional shock, physical trauma, or an overwhelming spiritual event, it is common, according to this view, for a part of their soul to detach as a form of self-protection. This fragmented part, driven by the survival instinct, isolates itself in some spiritual dimension, awaiting the moment it will be sought, recognized, and reintegrated. This partial soul loss is known as *soul loss*, and it is among the most central concepts of shamanic spiritual medicine. What the West calls deep depression, existential emptiness, extreme apathy, or self-sabotaging behavior, shamanism interprets as the unequivocal sign that something has been lost. The person is no longer whole. They are living with only a part of their vital energy.

And the most frightening thing: this fragmented part can gain its own life. It doesn't disappear—it persists, in a state of suspension, living with limited consciousness somewhere on the astral plane. In doing so, it becomes something very similar to what we call in this study an astral clone: a spiritual duplicate, semi-autonomous, generated from trauma and sustained by an invisible bond with the originator.

This fragment can take symbolic forms in the spiritual worlds explored by the shaman. Sometimes, it appears as a frightened child locked in a cave. In other cases, as a wounded animal, a broken object, or even a shadow fleeing contact. These images are archetypal representations of what the dissociated part is experiencing. For the shaman, these fragments have emotions, memories, and their own will. They may resist returning, fearing to relive the original pain. And when this happens, they become spiritual doubles—parts of the original self walking alone, wandering through the invisible worlds, subtly affecting the incarnated individual, who feels its effects without knowing their origin.

In some South American shamanic traditions, such as among the peoples of the Amazon, it is believed that these lost soul parts can be captured by forest entities or dark spirits. These beings exploit the fragment's vibrational fragility and imprison it, using its energy as food or a tool. Thus, the astral clone, already a piece of the being itself, comes to be manipulated by external intelligences. The bond with the original remains, but the influence becomes perverse: the individual begins to feel anxieties, nightmares, energetic illnesses, and existential blocks that seem causeless. They are being affected from a distance by their own shadow, now serving another master.

Shamanism offers ways to deal with this. The most powerful and transformative is the so-called *soul retrieval ritual*. In it, the shaman enters a trance—usually induced by the rhythmic sound of the drum, rattle, or voice—and travels to the spiritual realms in search of the patient's lost fragments. This journey can last minutes or hours, and is not without spiritual dangers. Often, the shaman must confront symbolic guardians, overcome archetypal obstacles, and convince the fragment to return. When found, they welcome it, heal it with breaths, chants, and intentions, and bring it back to the person's body, usually blowing it into their heart, head, or solar plexus.

The experience of soul retrieval is profoundly transformative. Many patients report feelings of reconnection, peace, tears without reason, vivid dreams of parts of themselves returning. Over time, they recover energy, clarity, and purpose. In terms of the phenomenon we investigate, the trauma-originated astral clone is dissolved by reintegration: it ceases to be a separate entity because it returns to the totality of the being.

However, there is another type of spiritual duplication recognized in shamanic practices—one that is not born from trauma, but from the shaman's will. In many cultures, it is believed that the experienced sorcerer or shaman is capable of creating and sending their "nagual," or spiritual double, to act at a distance. This duplicate can take human, animal, or even elemental forms. It is used for healings, protection, spiritual investigations, or, in dark cases, for attacks and spells. Here, we have a direct parallel with the intentional creation of astral clones as described in Chaos Magic. The difference is that, in shamanism, this process is ancestral, symbolic, and deeply ritualized.

When creating their nagual, the shaman imprints part of their soul onto a symbolic form, fed with vital energy and clear purposes. This double, however, remains linked to them. Its existence depends on the bond and ritual maintenance. If not reabsorbed or dissolved after use, it can escape, wander, become corrupted. Some ancient accounts tell of shamans driven mad after losing control of their doubles, which began acting on their own, creating chaos in the invisible worlds and earthly planes. In these cases, what was a sacred tool becomes an uncontrolled astral clone—a spiritual copy without command, influenced by non-human forces and dangerously free.

Shamanic traditions, therefore, warn of the risks of irresponsible unfolding. The human soul, though multiple by nature, is delicate in its integrity. Every fragment that moves away represents not only energy loss but also loss of memory, will, and protection. Excessive fragmentation can leave the being vulnerable to obsessors, illnesses, bad luck, and existential disorientation. The astral clone, as a reflection of this fragmentation, is both a symptom and an agent of disharmony. It cries out for return, but may resist. It seeks its home, but may have already been seduced by other forces. The shaman's work is to guide it back, with wisdom, strength, and love.

It is notable that many accounts of possession, bilocation, spectral apparitions, and altered states of consciousness described in shamanic contexts coincide with phenomena studied in modern esoteric schools under the name "astral duplication." The language changes, the symbol varies, but the core of the experience remains: the human being can unfold, fragment, and even duplicate energetically. And when this happens involuntarily, the result can be a semi-autonomous entity—the astral clone—that subtly interferes in the originator's life, even if they ignore its existence.

The shamanic response to this is simple, yet profound: return to the center. Reintegration. Reconnection with the Earth, with ancestors, with natural rhythms. The shaman does not see the clone as an enemy, but as a call. A warning that something is out of place. And its healing is not done with violent expulsions or dogmas, but with listening, with dances, with dreams, and with humility before the Mystery. The astral clone, from the shamanic perspective, is more than a phenomenon—it is a disguised master. It shows where the being got lost. And its dissolution is not an end, but a rebirth: the return of the fragment to the whole, of the exiled to home, of pain to wholeness. And the drum continues to sound, guiding the way back home.

Chapter 8
Spiritist View

The Spiritist Doctrine offers a comprehensive and sensitive interpretation of the invisible dynamics governing the interaction between the incarnate spirit and the multiple manifestations of the spiritual plane. Founded on teachings transmitted by higher spirits and organized by Allan Kardec, this view understands the human being as an eternal spirit in a continuous process of evolution, temporarily clothed in a physical body and a semi-material envelope called the perispirit. This, in turn, acts as the link between the dense and subtle planes, functioning as the energetic mold of the carnal body and, at the same time, as the vehicle for expressing spiritual individuality in states of unfolding, sleep, disincarnation, or disturbance. Within this field of possibilities, the existence of spiritual duplications, or perispiritual fragmentations, is recognized as a legitimate phenomenon—albeit uncommon and complex—which can be understood in light of Spiritist principles as a consequence of emotional imbalances, obsessive influences, or specific karmic conditions.

The malleability of the perispirit, its sensitivity to mental vibrations, and its ability to project onto multiple dimensional levels make it susceptible to involuntary unfoldings or accidental fragmentations. When intense emotional shocks, spiritual traumas, or prolonged patterns of mental negativity occur, certain portions of the perispirit can partially detach from the integral structure, assuming autonomous or semi-autonomous forms on the spiritual plane. These forms, imbued with dense psychic content—such as resentment, anger, fear, or desire for revenge—begin to act as conscious or semi-conscious entities, often manifesting with appearance, voice, and personality similar to the originator. Contemporary spiritualist literature has associated the term astral clone with these manifestations, understanding them as derivations of the being itself, actively maintained by fluidic connections, unresolved emotional memories, and, in many cases, exploited by lower spiritual intelligences.

Spiritism, when analyzing this type of occurrence, does not classify it as an external anomaly or an isolated attack, but as an amplified reflection of the incarnate spirit's inner state. Obsession, in its most complex form, often involves subtle structures that go beyond the simple connection between obsessor and obsessed: they include perispiritual duplications molded from the victim's own vibrational field. These materialized thought-forms, endowed with relative autonomy, can act as instruments of spiritual domination, mental interference, and energetic depletion. However, the Spiritist approach emphasizes that such manifestations are neither definitive nor invincible. They represent, above all, an opportunity for learning, moral rebalancing, and liberation. Spiritual healing occurs through raising the mental frequency, inner renewal, and the constant practice of good. Thus, even facing the phenomenon of the astral clone, the Spiritist Doctrine reaffirms its fundamental conviction: the human spirit is always master of its destiny and holds the power to regenerate itself through love, consciousness, and inner reform.

Allan Kardec, codifier of Spiritism, when organizing the foundations of the doctrine based on communications from higher spirits, did not directly use the expression "astral clone." However, the principles he established allow for understanding the possibility of spiritual duplications or unfoldings of the perispirit—the semi-material envelope linking the spirit to the physical body. This perispirit, being malleable and susceptible to the individual's mental and emotional emanations, can, under certain conditions, be manipulated or fragmented. Thus, the phenomenon of the astral clone can be interpreted as a degenerate form of unfolding or as an artifact resulting from deep obsessions.

The perispirit, according to the Spiritist Doctrine, is the intermediary between spirit and matter. It serves as the mold for the physical body, but also as the vehicle for the spirit's expression when disincarnate or unfolded. During sleep, for example, it is common for the spirit to partially withdraw from the physical body, remaining connected by a fluidic link known as the silver cord. In this condition, it can act in the spiritual world, meet other spirits, receive instructions, or even participate in rescue activities. However, in some cases, due to traumas, disturbances, or spiritual attacks, this unfolding can generate semi-independent forms—duplicates that remain activated even after the spirit's partial return to the physical body.

It is here that modern spiritualist research, especially in the field of apometry and mediumship of disobsession, begins to shed light on astral clones. In Brazilian Spiritist and spiritualist centers, many mediums report cases of obsession where the manifesting entity is not actually a disincarnate spirit, but a form extracted from the victim's own perispirit. This form has the appearance, voice, and even mannerisms of the person, but acts against them. It's as if a fragment of the self has been hijacked, programmed, and transformed into a spiritual puppet, used by obsessors or dark magicians to influence the victim's life subtly and continuously.

In the book "Lords of Darkness," of mediumistic authorship, an operation carried out by highly specialized obsessing spirits is described, who extract portions of their victims' astral bodies during sleep or states of disturbance. These portions are molded into astral duplicates—true clones—which are kept in dark spiritual laboratories. There, these clones are hypnotized, conditioned, and then reconnected to the incarnate's mind through a fluidic connection. The result is devastating: the individual begins to have thoughts that are not their own, distorted feelings, disturbing dreams, and often illnesses that defy medical diagnosis.

This type of obsession is known as complex subjugation. It involves not only the presence of a disturbing spirit but an entire fluidic engineering that transforms parts of the victim's own being into instruments of their spiritual imprisonment. The astral clone, in this context, is a link between the obsessor and the obsessed—a bridge of interference, a psychic Trojan horse operating within the person's energetic structure, sabotaging their will, draining their vitality, and disturbing their peace.

Apometry, a technique developed by José Lacerda de Azevedo, and later refined by various spiritualist groups, has proven particularly effective in identifying and treating these cases. Through the conscious unfolding of mediums and the use of specific verbal commands, facilitators can locate astral clones, identify their links, and promote their dissolution or reintegration. In many accounts, the clones appear confused, like zombies or spiritual automatons, without full awareness of their origin. When they understand they are fragments of the person and not independent spirits, they undergo energetic collapse and are reabsorbed or disintegrated, depending on the case.

In traditional Spiritist centers, the treatment of deep obsessions involves magnetic passes, prayers, Gospel study at home, mental harmonization, and continuous monitoring of the victim. Although the language is more symbolic and less technical than in apometry, the effects are similar: over time, the person's energy field clears, harmful fluidic connections weaken, and the influence of the astral clone, if present, is reduced until it disappears.

It is important to highlight that, in the Spiritist view, the existence of an astral clone is not a condemnation. It is seen as a consequence of a prior spiritual imbalance, often linked to recurring negative thoughts, uncontrolled emotions, or karmic debts. Therefore, the treatment is never just energetic or mediumistic—it is moral. The individual is guided to change their mental habits, elevate their thoughts, cultivate prayer, charity, and study. Only then is the root of the problem treated, and not just its effects.

There are also records of spontaneous manifestations of these astral clones during mediumistic sessions. Some entities presenting themselves as "obsessing spirits" are, in fact, animated thought-forms, created by the incarnate themselves. These forms, when manifesting through mediumship, reveal their origins: they are copies of anger, envy, fear, or desire for revenge, cast over the years and unconsciously fed. They appear with human appearance, speak, cry, complain, but their essence is energetic, not spiritual. The medium perceives them clearly, and the indoctrinators need to apply specific techniques to dissolve the link, demagnetize the form, and restore harmony to the person's field.

There is a point of profound wisdom in how Spiritism views these manifestations. Kardec always taught that spirits—and, by extension, any form of life on the subtle plane—are beings in evolution. This includes, therefore, the fragments of the human soul that, due to maladjustment or interference, take temporary life. The astral clone, however problematic, is part of the being's evolutionary process. It is the materialization of what was rejected, hidden, or unbalanced. Its dissolution should not be done with hatred or fear, but with light, understanding, and love.

Spiritism also teaches that no spiritual influence persists without the permission—albeit unconscious—of the incarnate. The astral clone, therefore, is not an invading entity, but a co-authorized creation. This implies responsibility and freedom: if we were capable of creating, we can also undo. If we fragmented ourselves, we can also reunite. And this is, perhaps, the greatest teaching of the Spiritist Doctrine on the subject: the human being is a co-creator of their destiny, on all planes. And even the shadows that arise on the path are invitations to growth, light, and reconciliation with oneself. The astral clone, then, is not an enemy, but a mirror. It shows what still needs to be healed, what still bleeds in the soul. And by facing it, with serenity and faith, we can, finally, find the way back to spiritual wholeness—step by step, prayer by prayer, light by light.

Chapter 9
Thought-Forms

The subtle reality permeating the human mental and emotional universe is composed of a vastness of forms shaped by the mind, emotions, and will. Each thought, upon being generated, projects itself as an energetic impulse that reverberates on the astral plane, carrying with it the vibrational essence of its origin. When this emission is occasional or weak, it dissipates quickly, like a breeze in the wind. However, when the thought is charged with intense emotion, reiterated frequently, and sustained by vivid mental images, it gains density and form, crystallizing as an active vibrational entity—the thought-form. This becomes not just a symbolic reflection of its creator, but an agent with a certain energetic autonomy, capable of interfering in the emotional, mental, and spiritual field of the individual or those to whom it is directed.

It is in this unconscious and continuous creative process that the origin of what may later be recognized as an astral clone is found. The genesis of the astral clone is rooted in repetition and emotional intensity. Unlike simpler thought-forms, which represent only fleeting ideas or punctual emotions, the astral clone is an entity molded from deeply ingrained and recurring internal contents. It is the result of prolonged symbolic accumulation—a psychic image that, by being fed by persistent emotional patterns, acquires structural complexity. It is a sophisticated energetic configuration, containing fragments of the creator's memory, identity, motivations, and even self-image. Upon reaching this level of cohesion, the thought-form ceases to be merely a projection and transforms into an autonomous reflection: a symbiotic spiritual duplicate, interacting with the astral reality and, in many cases, acting as a dissociated extension of the being itself.

This phenomenon manifests more frequently in individuals who, for various reasons—traumas, repressions, intense desires, or prolonged internal conflicts—end up projecting parts of the psyche outside the conscious field. The mind, unable to integrate certain contents, seeks to alleviate them through symbolic externalization, creating forms that, over time, become independent. Thus, the thought-form evolves into an astral clone, carrying not only the original emotion but also the desire for continuity and preservation. This creation is not necessarily malignant. It is, rather, a psychic response to an internal collapse, an unconscious attempt to maintain cohesion through fragmentation. Understanding this dynamic is fundamental to addressing not only the dissolution of these entities but also the need for emotional and psychic restructuring that their existence denounces.

The creation of thought-forms is a constant phenomenon, although imperceptible to most. Every thought generated by a human being carries within it a vibration, an energetic signature. When this thought is fleeting or superficial, it dissipates almost instantly. But when it is repeated, reinforced by intense emotion—be it love, fear, anger, envy, or desire—and sustained by concentration or habit, it begins to condense on the astral plane. The subtle matter, which is extremely plastic there, molds itself according to the symbolic and emotional content of the emitted idea. The result is a temporary entity that remains active as long as it receives energy from its creator.

These thought-forms can assume infinite appearances, depending on their emotional content and the imagery of the one who emitted them. A thought of protection might manifest as a shield, an angel, a luminous sphere. A thought of hatred might take the form of a monster, a knife, or a fierce animal. They have color, form, movement, and even a kind of rudimentary instinctive intelligence. Some are intentionally sent to other people, as in cases of mental magic or psychic vampirism. Others simply orbit the creator's energy field, silently influencing them with the same vibrations that generated them.

Esoteric literature describes thought-forms of various levels of complexity. There are the simplest ones, created by punctual thoughts and sporadic emotions. They are like mental sparks that extinguish quickly. There are intermediate ones, formed through recurring mental habits—a pattern of criticism, fear, or desire, for example—which remain in the individual's auric field like true vibrational clouds, affecting their mood, health, and mental clarity. And finally, there are complex thought-forms: entities created from intense and prolonged feelings, allied with vivid mental images and sustained over time. It is in this last group that the astral clone fits.

It is a thought-form of extremely high complexity, a condensed fragment of the psyche itself, which has crystallized so densely on the astral plane that it began to act as a spiritual copy. Unlike common thought-forms, the clone carries not just one emotion or idea, but a structured set of memories, patterns, behaviors, and images of the creator themselves. It is, so to speak, a symbiotic entity, born of repetition, desire, and pain, and sustained by an energetic link that remains as long as the original emotional pattern is not transformed.

This process is especially common in people experiencing deep internal conflicts. When an aspect of personality is repressed—a desire, a memory, an unaccepted emotion—it does not disappear. On the contrary, it tends to project outward, seeking a symbolic space where it can exist. If this aspect is fed with intensity, it gains form. And if sustained consistently, this form becomes autonomous. This is how, unintentionally, many create astral clones: by projecting outward parts of their psychic shadow that they cannot bear to face.

In Eastern traditions, particularly in Tibetan Buddhism, there is the notion of *tulpas*—beings formed by the human mind with such vigor that they acquire their own existence. These mental constructs can be positive or negative, depending on the creator's intention. An advanced practitioner might create a tulpa to help them on their spiritual journey, as a guardian or meditation companion. However, there are reports of tulpas that escaped the creator's control, acquiring independent traits, resisting dissolution, and even interfering in the creator's life. It's the same principle as the astral clone: a thought-form so dense and structured that it surpasses the role of reflection and becomes an entity with its own agency.

In Western occult schools, especially Theosophy and Chaos Magic, the study of thought-forms is one of the bases for understanding mental magic. The operator learns to generate, feed, program, and dissolve these forms. But they are also warned about the risks of creating them unconsciously. A thought of self-deprecation, repeated daily and reinforced by negative emotions, can become a dark thought-form that fixes itself in the solar plexus chakra and begins to sabotage all self-worth initiatives. An obsessive desire for revenge, for example, can generate a rancorous astral clone that wanders the astral plane trying to symbolically harm the target—and returning to the creator with unpredictable vibrational consequences.

The problem worsens when these thought-forms find affinity with entities of the lower astral plane. Astral larvae and other opportunistic beings, upon perceiving the presence of an intense vibrational form, approach, feed on it, and, in some cases, merge with it. The astral clone, in these cases, becomes hybrid: part creator, part obsessor. This union generates an even more complex being, difficult to dissolve, as it no longer responds only to the creator, but also to other influences.

This is why some clones seem resistant to prayers, energetic baths, and reintegration attempts. They have already transformed into composite entities, requiring specific spiritual interventions for their dissolution.

Understanding thought-forms also allows one to grasp individual energetic responsibility. Thoughts are not harmless. Emotions are not neutral. Each vibrational emission creates waves in the fabric of the subtle plane, and these waves can condense into forms. The astral clone, however frightening it may seem, is merely the culmination of an unconscious creation process that occurred over time. It is a mirror that says: "This is how you thought. This is how you felt. This is what you created." And like any creation, it can be undone—not by denial, but by transformation.

Dissolving an astral clone therefore requires more than external rituals. It demands internal change. The source of its nourishment—the obsessive thought, the repressed emotion, the negative pattern—needs to be interrupted. The psyche must be reorganized. The individual must take command of their own mental and emotional field. Only then does the bond break. When the energy source ceases, the thought-form begins to naturally unravel, like a candle extinguishing without fuel.

The astral clone is a thought-form taken to its maximum degree of complexity. It carries the colors of emotion, the shape of thought, and the density of habit. And although it seems like an external entity, it is, in fact, an extension of the being itself. A child of the mind, a product of the soul in disharmony. Recognizing it as such is the first step to dissolving it. And dissolving it is, ultimately, reconnecting with a part of oneself that asks for light, consciousness, and reintegration.

Chapter 10
Internal Causes

The formation of an astral clone, when analyzed from the perspective of internal causes, reveals a profound process of psychic fragmentation operating silently in the subtlest layers of the being. Unlike explanations attributing such occurrences to external influences or spiritual manipulations by third parties, this approach focuses on the individual's intimate universe, where unresolved emotions, crystallized mental patterns, and unconscious conflicts form the vibrational brew conducive to generating astral duplicates. The clone, in this context, is a direct product of the creator themselves, a condensed extension of contents that were not adequately welcomed, processed, or integrated. It emerges as a reflection of the pain that was not felt, the desire that could not be lived, the identity that was repressed. By understanding this dynamic, it becomes possible not only to recognize the genesis of the duplication but also to build a real and effective path for its reintegration.

Repressed emotions play a central role in this process. When intense feelings like guilt, envy, fear, or resentment are systematically avoided or denied, the psyche does not nullify them—it stores them, encapsulates them, and eventually projects them outside the conscious field. This projection, repeatedly fed, gives rise to a symbolic form carrying the vibrational frequency of the original content. Such a form can develop silently for years, going unnoticed, until it reaches sufficient density to interact perceptibly with the mental or emotional field. This interaction manifests as sensations of internal conflict, self-sabotaging behaviors, identity disturbances, or even vivid dreams with figures personifying rejected aspects of the self. Contrary to what is often assumed, the clone's emergence is not sudden: it is the result of a continuous process of unconscious energetic feeding.

Another decisive element lies in the relationship between the idealized self and the personal shadow. The attempt to maintain a socially, spiritually, or morally acceptable image can lead to the violent exclusion of legitimate parts of the psyche which, although uncomfortable, make up the individual's whole. These parts, relegated to the unconscious, begin seeking symbolic means of expression—and the astral plane offers a conducive field for this. The astral clone, in this case, emerges as the bearer of what was exiled: denied desires, unrecognized fears, unprocessed drives. Its existence is a warning: it carries the messages the ego refused to hear. Seeing it as an enemy only reinforces the internal division; recognizing it as part of the self-defense and self-preservation process is the first step to dissolving it. The return to unity requires this loving listening to what the soul tried to silence.

The first aspect to consider is deep, unresolved emotions. Contained anger, chronic sadness, ingrained resentments, fears cultivated in silence—all these forces vibrate intensely in the astral body. When these emotions remain active for prolonged periods, they generate zones of instability in the subtle field. These zones, in turn, become energetic vortices that attract, condense, and eventually expel parts of consciousness as a form of self-protection. The individual can no longer sustain that energy within themselves, and so it is projected outward, creating a symbolic entity—an astral clone carrying the vibrational content the originator failed to integrate.

This process can be subtle. Imagine a person who, for years, nurtures a desire to escape their own reality. They dream of being someone else, living another life, leaving everything behind. Initially, this seems harmless. But the mind, by repeating such desires with emotional intensity, begins to shape a psychic reflection. This reflection organizes itself on the astral plane as a duplicate representing this "desired version" of the person. The clone is born as a kind of unconscious avatar of the desire for evasion. Over time, this duplicate begins to manifest in dreams, interfere with decisions, induce feelings of dissatisfaction, and amplify the sense of inadequacy. All this because a piece of consciousness was projected—and now acts with relative autonomy.

Another risk factor is the conflict between persona and shadow. The persona is the social face, the image the individual projects to the world—controlled, functional, morally acceptable. The shadow, in turn, is the set of desires, impulses, and characteristics that have been repressed or judged unacceptable. When this conflict intensifies, the astral field suffers. The repressed part, denied by consciousness, tends to seek expression somehow. And since the psychic field cannot tolerate vacuums, what is not integrated tends to shift outward. Thus, an astral clone emerges carrying the shadow's content—often with a distorted appearance, aggressive or instinctual behavior, and a propensity to cause emotional or spiritual sabotage.

Analytical psychology, when dealing with the shadow, speaks of the need to integrate it into the conscious self to avoid destructive projections. On the spiritual plane, this means recognizing that the astral clone is not an enemy, but a messenger. It reveals what has not yet been accepted. Its mere existence points to a blind spot, a corner of the soul crying out for recognition. And ignoring it only increases its power, as what is rejected tends to grow in the darkness.

Poorly conducted spiritual practices can also generate astral clones due to internal causes. When a person engages in meditation, astral projection, invocations, or other esoteric techniques without proper emotional and mental preparation, they risk activating areas of the psyche not yet ready to be released. For example, someone seeking regular out-of-body experiences but carrying unhealed traumas might project a fragment of themselves that, once released, cannot easily return. This fragment, fed by fear or desire, can crystallize as an astral clone. And contrary to what the practitioner thinks, they are not just exploring higher planes—they are losing parts of themselves in the process.

This loss, although subtle, manifests in concrete symptoms. A sense of existential emptiness, unexplained energy loss, difficulty concentrating, recurring dreams of an "other self," a feeling of not being alone within one's own mind—all are indications that something has fragmented. The clone, in this scenario, is not an external attack, but the echo of a practice done without discernment, anchoring, or necessary guidance.

A particularly delicate point is repressed desires. Many astral clones originate from intense impulses consciously rejected. Sexual desires, ambitions for power, feelings of superiority or revenge—all these contents, when repressed by morality, fear, or shame, do not disappear. They seek alternative ways to exist. And on the astral plane, they can condense as spiritual duplicates. These clones are often the hardest to accept, as they reveal aspects the individual does not want to recognize as their own. But they are, at the same time, those most urgently needing to be looked at, understood, and reintegrated.

There are also cases where the astral clone forms through a mechanism of psychological compensation. People who suffered profound losses—such as the death of loved ones, romantic frustrations, or emotional collapses—may unconsciously create duplicates to "replace" the lost part. The mind, in its effort to avoid suffering, creates another self that feels no pain, that is strong, that continues even when the original person wants to stop. This clone might seem like an ally, but over time reveals itself as a burden. It imposes patterns, demands control, sucks energy. After all, it was created to endure what the creator did not want to face. But no substitution lasts forever—and the price of keeping an emotional clone active is too high for the soul.

Thus, we can perceive that the internal causes of the astral clone's emergence are not just mistakes—they are defense mechanisms of the unconscious. They are the soul's attempts to maintain integrity amidst chaos. But these attempts, when unrecognized, eventually become prisons. The clone transforms into the silent jailer preventing true growth, as it keeps energy trapped in the past, in trauma, in the unresolved pattern.

Healing begins with recognition. Admitting that the astral clone was created from internal pain is the first step. Then, the energy source maintaining it must be deactivated. This requires courage to face what was denied: the unfelt emotion, the forbidden desire, the painful memory. In many cases, spiritual therapies are necessary—but so are psychological ones. For the astral clone is not just a spiritual problem; it is a symptom of the psyche. It shows where fragmentation lies. And only self-knowledge can restore the lost unity.

The path, therefore, is not of combat, but of reintegration. The astral clone, when seen with eyes of wisdom, becomes a teacher. It shows what needs healing. It brings to the surface what was buried. And by being understood, welcomed, and dissolved, it returns to the individual what was taken from them: wholeness, clarity, sovereignty over oneself.

Chapter 11
External Causes

Astral duplication provoked by external agents represents one of the most unsettling and dangerous manifestations of the energetic phenomenon. It emerges not as a consequence of the individual's internal conflicts or emotional maladjustments, but as the result of deliberate actions conducted by other consciousnesses, operating with the specific intent to manipulate, subjugate, or psychically exploit the victim. In this dynamic, the astral clone is a construction architected outside the host's will, utilizing subtle breaches in their energy field. This intervention respects no boundaries between the visible and invisible worlds and manifests with sophisticated strategies that challenge the ordinary perception of reality. The victim, often, is completely unaware that part of their energy has been hijacked and molded by external intelligences for obscure purposes. This is a phenomenon that transcends simple spiritual influence, entering the field of occult engineering applied to the subtle body.

The forces promoting this type of invasion are neither casual nor improvised. They operate based on accumulated knowledge and techniques refined over millennia, found in occult traditions, spiritualist doctrines, and ancestral accounts from distinct civilizations. Obsessing spirits, negative magicians, and entities from the lower astral are examples of these agents who precisely manipulate aspects of the human perispirit, creating duplicates that function as mechanisms of interference and control. The intention behind these creations ranges from energetic draining to inducing mental and emotional states that weaken discernment and reduce the person's spiritual resistance. Instead of acting directly on the individual, these consciousnesses use the astral clone as a vibrational bridge, remaining hidden while exerting continuous and profound influence over their victim.

The impact of these external duplications is devastating precisely because of its subtlety. The victim may feel extreme fatigue, lapses of consciousness, emotional and spiritual distortions, and even a sense of not belonging to their own body or mind. However, without physical or logical evidence explaining these symptoms, they tend to attribute them to daily stress, psychological problems, or transient disturbances. This further amplifies the entities' dominance, as the greater the ignorance about what is really happening, the greater the effectiveness of the control exerted. The clone, in this context, is not just an energetic replica: it is a tool of conscious manipulation, precisely designed to occupy sensitive spaces in the person's vibrational field, interrupting higher spiritual connections and establishing a pattern of continuous imbalance. Recognizing the existence of these external causes is the first step towards reclaiming spiritual autonomy and energetic sovereignty.

One of the most recurrent forms of external creation of astral clones occurs through the action of obsessing spirits. These beings, discarnate entities trapped in lower planes due to attachment, anger, ignorance, or perversity, develop complex techniques of psychic domination. It's not about simple vibrational approximations or telepathic inductions. In many cases, it involves actual surgical interventions on the victim's perispirit. The obsessor, identifying an emotional or energetic vulnerability, uses this entry point to manipulate parts of the astral body. And with adequate knowledge, can extract, duplicate, or mold a part of the victim's perispirit into an astral clone under their command.

This clone, although carrying the appearance and vibrational signature of the original, is no longer under their control. It becomes an extension of the obsessor's will, functioning like a spiritual puppet. The victim, often unknowingly, begins to be influenced by impulses they don't recognize as their own, suffers from inexplicable exhaustion, intense emotional oscillations, lapses of consciousness, and even behavioral changes. The clone, in this context, acts as an intermediary, a channel of action between the obsessor and the victim's mind. And because it was molded from the host's own essence, it has deep access to their fears, memories, and mental patterns.

In spiritualist centers and apometry groups, this type of case is described as a process of "fluidic cloning," where a part of the person's astral body is separated, molded, and programmed by spiritual entities. Some of these entities are true "technologists of the lower astral," spirits highly specialized in manipulating energy, implanting devices, and creating sophisticated forms of dominion. They operate with precision and discretion, often without the victim having any awareness of what is happening. The generated clone is then linked to the original by hidden energetic cords, allowing not only energy draining but also the insertion of thoughts, feelings, and impulses.

Another field of action for external causes is negative magic. Within practices of malicious witchcraft, perverted goetia, and sorcery aimed at psychic domination, there are specific rituals for creating astral duplicates of a person. One of the oldest methods is the use of symbolic dolls—the so-called voodoo dolls—where the magician uses elements of the target (hair, nails, photographs, used clothes) to establish a vibrational connection. From this link, and with appropriate rituals, it is possible to construct an astral form resembling the victim, which then serves as their spiritual substitute. This duplicate is then used as a receptacle for commands, curses, or influences that, through vibrational sympathy, affect the original.

Such practices are ancient and universal. Similar records exist in African, European, Asian, and indigenous cultures. All share the notion that it is possible to act on a person from a distance by manipulating a representation of them. In the case of the astral clone, this representation is not just symbolic, but energetic. The duplicate, once created, gains its own life on the subtle plane, directly influencing the target's vibrational field. The person begins to experience psychic and physical symptoms without apparent cause: mental confusion, a sense of invasion, strange dreams, constant fatigue, a drop in sexual and vital energy, among others.

In many cases, the astral clone created by negative magic acts as a barrier between the victim and their spiritual guides. It blocks intuition, distorts messages received in dreams or meditations, and creates a field of interference that hinders contact with the higher plane. Furthermore, it functions as an anchoring point for other entities. Once the clone is connected to the original, it becomes an access route for obsessors, astral vampires, and other predatory consciousnesses. These entities feed on the energy generated by constant tension, negative emotions, and mental confusion caused by the clone's presence.

There are also cases where the clone is implanted in people who frequent environments of low spiritual vibration: places where dubious rituals are performed, sessions of selfish magic, or meetings with hidden intentions. In these environments, energies are dense, and if the person is weakened or inattentive, they can be "marked" by an entity that, over time, will extract a part of their energy to form a clone. This clone then remains lurking, often installed in the person's own energy field or in a specific environment. The person begins to feel drained, unstable, as if "outside themselves." And they are—because a part of them has been separated and is being used against them.

It is important to highlight that these external causes can only act when there is an internal breach. No one is completely vulnerable to spiritual attacks without having, on some level, opened space for it. Maintained anger, unresolved resentment, desire for revenge, envy, excessive pride—all these feelings create fissures in the energy field. And it is these fissures that negative magicians and obsessors exploit. Thus, even when the astral clone is created from outside, it only binds to the original because it finds resonance. External manipulation always finds an internal echo that sustains it.

Dissolving these clones requires a multifaceted approach. It is necessary to cleanse the energy field, cut vibrational links, undo mental commands, and restore the integrity of the astral body. In spiritualist centers, this is done through passes, prayers, use of herbs, smudging, apometric treatments, regressions, and protection techniques. In white magic rituals, alchemical transmutation of energy, raising vibrational frequency, and invoking higher forces are used to undo the created bonds. The fundamental thing is to understand that the clone is not just an entity—it is a link. And cutting this link requires both external action and internal transformation.

The victim also needs to take their part in the process. They need to rebalance their thoughts, purify their emotions, cut harmful habits, and strengthen their spirituality. Without this change, even if the clone is dissolved, another could be created. Vigilance is continuous. Energetic integrity is not a state, but a daily practice. And as the person strengthens, the possibilities of interference decrease drastically.

    The external causes of astral clone creation remind us that the spiritual universe is a dynamic field of relationships. There are forces that want to elevate us and forces that want to imprison us. But free will is always ours. Even facing the subtlest manipulations, awakened consciousness is capable of undoing any knot. The astral clone, even when created by others, is not invincible. It is a shadow molded by artifice. And every shadow, however dense, dissolves in the presence of light. This light, which is inner truth, soul strength, mental clarity, and heart purity, is the only weapon that never fails. The clone dissolves. The bond breaks. And the being returns to the center of their own light.

Chapter 12
Trauma and Fragmentation

The impact of deep trauma extends beyond the boundaries of emotional suffering and reverberates throughout the multidimensional structure of the being, instigating a fragmentation process that compromises psychic and spiritual integrity. When pain reaches an unbearable threshold, the internal system instinctively resorts to self-protection mechanisms involving the isolation of parts of consciousness. These portions, impregnated with the emotional charge of the traumatic event, do not disappear—they detach from the core self and begin to exist autonomously in the subtle planes, creating energetic duplicates that retain the memories, feelings, and beliefs associated with the original experience. This process of fission, operating silently in the deep layers of the psyche, gives rise to astral fragments that function like satellites of pain: they orbit the central consciousness, influence decisions, shape reactions, and perpetuate patterns of suffering.

These fragments are not just emotional reminiscences; they become subtle forms with their own identity, developing a certain behavioral and energetic autonomy. By establishing themselves on the astral plane, they acquire characteristics that make them perceptible in altered states of consciousness, such as meditations, lucid dreams, and regression practices. They often assume symbolic appearances directly linked to the type of trauma experienced—representations that, even if not immediately recognized by the conscious mind, carry the hidden truth of unprocessed pain.

The phenomenon of duplication, in this context, is not the product of deliberate intent, but an inevitable consequence of the unconscious attempt to contain pain. It's as if the soul, to survive, had to leave parts of itself behind, in chambers sealed in time. These energetic duplicates, formed under the sign of suffering, become recurring and persistent influences in daily life. They attract events similar to those that gave rise to them, recreate contexts of pain, sabotage relationships, and impede the realization of higher purposes. Not as punishment, but as an unconscious attempt at reintegration, at closing cycles. By manifesting as conflicting internal forces or disproportionate emotional states, these psychic clones denounce the existence of a wounded core crying out for attention. More than symptoms, they are living expressions of a plea for healing. The presence of these fragments does not indicate weakness, but the depth of human experience—and points precisely to where the key to true inner transformation lies.

Spiritual fragmentation caused by trauma is a phenomenon recognized in multiple traditions. Shamanism speaks of soul loss: when a part of the being departs to avoid facing the experienced horror. Western esotericism speaks of traumatic unfolding, where portions of consciousness separate from the whole, originating semi-autonomous entities. Transpersonal psychology recognizes the existence of subpersonalities or dissociative complexes that take control of the individual in moments of crisis. In all these cases, the language varies, but the core of the experience remains: intense trauma has the power to break the being into pieces.

When a trauma is not integrated—whether due to lack of support, emotional repression, or unconscious defense mechanisms—it becomes encapsulated. The memory of the event, the associated emotion, and the part of the self that experienced it are isolated from the main consciousness. What remains is a frozen fragment, continuing to exist in a remote point of the psyche or, more frequently, on the astral plane. This fragment, over time, can acquire characteristics of autonomy: it begins to have its own reactions, desires, patterns, and even symbolic forms. It becomes, in effect, an astral clone—a piece of the person living outside them, eternally re-enacting the moment of original pain.

Many of these clones do not appear with the exact appearance of the creator. They manifest as frightened children, angry adolescents, weeping women, violent men—figures representing the traumatized aspect of the psyche. They are parts stuck in time, frozen at the frequency of suffering. And when these duplicates become conscious on the astral plane, they begin to interfere in the individual's life. They attract situations similar to those that originated the trauma, in an unconscious attempt at resolution. They create repetitive patterns of failure, abuse, abandonment, rejection. They are like echoes of the past refusing to die.

It is important to understand that these manifestations are not enemies. They are cries for help. They are pieces of the soul crying out for acceptance, recognition, love. The trauma-generated astral clone is, in essence, a living symbol of unhealed pain. It carries the energy of the event, the weight of repressed emotion, the burden of limiting beliefs formed on that occasion. And as long as it is not reintegrated, it will continue to influence the person's energy field, draining their vitality, interfering in relationships, sabotaging projects, and distorting their self-perception.

These clones, being deeply linked to emotions of suffering, tend to fixate on specific regions of the energy body—especially the solar plexus (center of emotions), the heart (center of affective pains), and the throat (center of expression). It is common for the person to feel inexplicable physical pain in these areas, or sensations of weight, blockage, heat, or intense cold. Recurring dreams with versions of oneself in situations of suffering or conflict, or with symbolic figures that actually represent the clone seeking contact, are also frequent.

Many of these fragments assume a defensive posture. Accustomed to pain and abandonment, they resist reintegration. They manifest with hostility, distrust, or indifference. Therefore, aggressive approaches do not work. The dissolution of a traumatic astral clone is not achieved through combat, but through compassion. The healing work requires listening, presence, and empathy. One must look at the fragment with the eyes of a mother, father, faithful friend. Tell it: "I see you. I acknowledge your pain. You belong to me. Come home."

Regression therapies, inner child healing, guided visualizations, and shamanic soul retrieval practices are effective tools for this process. In these methods, the individual accesses the subtle planes of their consciousness and re-encounters the lost fragment. The encounter is often profoundly emotional. The person sees themselves in a younger version, in tears, in panic, or simply disconnected. The mere reconnection already initiates the healing process. But the next step—reintegration—requires intention, forgiveness, and commitment. Forgiving oneself for what could not be avoided. Releasing the retained emotion safely. Reprogramming the beliefs installed at that moment. All this is part of the work of dissolving the traumatic astral clone.

And, once completed, the effects are profound: emotional relief, mental clarity, a sense of presence, increased energy, and, above all, the perception of being whole again.

It is worth noting that, in more severe cases, the clone may have been co-opted by entities of the lower astral plane. This occurs when the fragment, vibrating in intense pain, attracts the attention of obsessors or negative thought-forms. These beings exploit the duplicate's fragility to feed it with negative emotions and use it as an access point to the creator's energy field. The clone then becomes a spiritual Trojan horse, facilitating the influence of external forces on the person. In these cases, besides emotional healing, specific spiritual work is necessary: banishments, energetic cleansings, apometry, magnetic passes, and invocations of protection.

However, even in these cases, the principle remains: the clone is a part of the person. And only they can ultimately authorize its dissolution. That is why regaining personal power is so important. By taking responsibility for their healing, the individual interrupts the energy flow sustaining the duplicate. By integrating the pain, they dissolve the form. And by welcoming the wounded part, they become stronger, more whole, more conscious.

Trauma fragments. But consciousness heals. The astral clone, although seemingly an enemy, is actually an invitation to reconcile with the past. It is the map of unresolved pain. And whoever has the courage to follow it to the end finds, at the center of the labyrinth, not a monster, but a frightened child. By embracing it, everything changes. The clone disappears. The shadow illuminates. And the being rediscovers itself, deeper, truer, fuller.

Chapter 13
Negative Magic

The intentional manipulation of subtle forces for destructive purposes reveals a dark facet of the interaction between consciousnesses on the astral plane. In the field of negative magic, each act is carefully architected to interfere with free will, sabotage harmony, and weaken the vital essence of the chosen target. The creation of astral clones within this context represents one of the most sophisticated and insidious strategies used by magicians acting in tune with involutive currents. These operators not only know the laws governing energy manipulation but also master specific techniques of fluidic duplication with the intent to subjugate, spy on, divert, or compromise the natural flow of the human soul. Unlike unconscious projections or fragments generated by trauma, the clone here is molded with intention and precision, functioning as a parasitic link between the magician and the victim.

The astral engineering involved in forming these clones is based on the deliberate use of elements vibrating in resonance with the victim. From collecting personal objects, biological residues, vibrational or astrological data, the magician establishes a direct bridge to the individual's subtle field. This connection, once activated, allows access and extraction of authentic energetic portions, which are then molded into a thinking form with its own structure and behavior. The resulting clone is not a mere symbolic copy—it is an active duplicate, programmed to operate as an extension of the magician's will. Its functions can range from causing emotional and mental disturbances to completely blocking the victim's access to their intuition, spiritual guides, or higher purpose. In some cases, it is installed as a barrier in the spiritual field; in others, as a direct channel of interference.

The real danger of these clones created by negative magic lies in their hybrid nature: they share the victim's vibrational signature but operate under external command. This gives the attack a high degree of camouflage and effectiveness. The alterations experienced by the person are confused with their own emotional issues, leading them to seek inadequate or ineffective solutions. They feel tired without reason, experience states of mental confusion, face sudden drops in energy, or are afflicted by destructive thoughts they don't recognize as their own. Gradually, their spiritual vitality is eroded, their will is weakened, and their self-perception becomes distorted. The clone thus becomes an agent of reprogramming, redirecting the soul's trajectory towards disorder, fear, and detachment from its higher essence. Identifying this manipulation is the first step to neutralizing it and restoring personal power.

It is necessary to understand that negative magic does not act randomly. It uses natural laws—the same laws governing white magic—but applies them for purposes contrary to the common good. The manipulation of thought-forms, intentional projection of energy, acting on the astral body of others, all fall within the scope of magical action. When an operator of negative magic chooses a target, they begin a meticulous process of vibrational analysis, identification of weak points, and collection of symbolic elements—such as photos, hair, personal objects, or even astrological and numerological information. These elements function as connection keys to the victim's energetic structure.

From this link, the magician begins constructing the astral clone. There are two main ways to do this: the first is by molding an energetic construct similar to the victim, infused with part of their original vibration; the second, more invasive, is through the direct extraction of fragments from the person's astral or mental body. This second path is more common in high-level magic cases, executed by initiates who deeply understand the mechanisms of fluidic duplication. For this, the magician might wait until the victim is asleep—when the astral body naturally separates from the physical—and then perform the "hijacking" of part of their energy.

This captured fragment is then molded with specific intentions. It can be programmed to transmit negative mental patterns, generate fear, insecurity, induce destructive behaviors, or even cause illnesses. The clone is endowed with partial autonomy and is kept active through periodic rituals, where the magician re-energizes the form, reaffirms its commands, and monitors its effects on the victim. In more extreme cases, the clone is placed as a barrier between the person and their own spirituality, functioning as a layer of interference that blocks intuition, hinders prayers, and interrupts the flow of energy with their guides and mentors.

The complexity of this manipulation lies in the fact that, since the clone is formed with material from the victim's own being, it possesses a legitimate connection with them. It is not an external entity invading their field, but an altered reflection of themselves. This is why it is so difficult to clearly identify the attack: the victim feels something is wrong, but cannot differentiate the imposed thoughts and emotions from those arising spontaneously.

The symptoms are subtle initially—recurrent fatigue, irritability, frequent nightmares, feelings of failure or helplessness. Over time, they intensify: panic attacks without apparent cause, a sense of persecution, memory loss, inexplicable professional or affective blocks. The symbolism of the "voodoo doll" is quite representative of this process. However, unlike the popular version, the astral clone is not just a physical representation of the victim. It is an active duplicate, inserted into the subtle plane, serving as a bridge between the magician and the original. Every action performed on the clone reverberates in the victim's physical, emotional, and mental body. If the magician inflicts pain on the duplicate, the target may feel physical symptoms; if they implant ideas into the clone, they may arise in the person's mind as intrusive thoughts. The victim may begin doubting themselves, lose willpower, develop addictions or compulsions they didn't previously have. The clone thus becomes a tool for negative spiritual reprogramming.

Besides individual use, there are also reports of occult organizations working with mass creation of astral clones for collective manipulation. Such groups, often linked to involutive currents of the spiritual plane, seek to generate duplicates of leaders, mediums, artists, or influential people, with the intent to weaken or divert them from their mission. These duplicates, when activated, interfere with the person's vibrational field, obscure their inner vision, and can even induce actions contrary to their ethics and purpose. When observing public figures who abruptly change behavior, lose their spiritual brightness, or get involved in inexplicable scandals, it is worth considering if there is interference from astral clones manipulated by negative magic.

In another aspect, there are magicians who create astral clones not to attack directly, but to spiritually spy on their victims. These duplicates are launched onto the subtle planes with the mission to observe, gather information, and transmit impressions to their creator. They are true astral spies, who can position themselves beside the person's bed during sleep, watch spiritual encounters, monitor meditative practices, or even interfere in healing sessions. Many mediums report having perceived, during unfoldings, distorted "versions" of themselves observing them from a distance. These presences are not always involuntary projections—sometimes, they are clones installed by third parties with well-defined purposes.

It is important to understand that the action of negative magic on the creation of astral clones is not restricted to a theoretical or mythological field. It is reported in apometry sessions, mediumistic sessions, shamanic consultations, and psychic investigations from various spiritual schools. And although reports vary in details and terminologies, the pattern is recurrent: someone loses a part of themselves, this part is manipulated by another, and the result is a deep fragmentation of spiritual identity.

Dissolving clones created by negative magic requires a careful and often multidisciplinary process. The first step is correct diagnosis—usually done by trained mediums or experienced spiritual therapists, who can identify the clone's presence, its nature, and its link to the magician. Next, it is necessary to cut the energetic cords linking the duplicate to the operator. This can be done with magnetic passes, verbal commands, banishing rituals, use of sacred symbols, or invocations of protection. After breaking the link, the clone can be dissolved—either by transmutation or reintegration, depending on its origin and nature.

However, the work doesn't end there. The most important thing is to seal the breach that allowed the intervention. This requires a deep review of the victim's emotional, mental, and spiritual life. What attitudes, thoughts, or feelings opened space for manipulation? Where was there self-neglect? What pacts, conscious or unconscious, allowed access? Only when these questions are answered and transformed will the protection become effective.

Negative magic feeds on fear, ignorance, and guilt. But when the light of consciousness is lit, it loses its power. The astral clone created by malicious intentions is just a shadow dependent on the continuation of darkness to survive. And when the being decides to look within, assume their sovereignty, and recover their wholeness, no spell can hold them. For the awakened soul, supported by its divine essence, is the greatest shield against any artifice of darkness. The clone dissolves. The bond breaks. And the being returns to the center of their own light.

Chapter 14
Energetic Bond

The subtle connections that interconnect all beings form an invisible web of energy in constant flow, where every thought, emotion, or act creates resonances that echo beyond the physical plane. Within this vibrational reality, no energetic creation exists in isolation. Every manifestation generated by a being, including astral clones, remains linked to its origin by a vibrational cord that acts as a dynamic channel of mutual influence. This energetic bond not only maintains the clone's existence but also establishes a feedback pathway between creator and creation, allowing the continuous exchange of impressions, information, and emotional patterns. The astral duplicate, therefore, is never a completely autonomous entity: it pulses with the original's energy, influences and is influenced, directly affecting the vitality, psychic balance, and spiritual trajectory of the one who generated it.

This energetic bridge functions like a circuit where the flow never ceases—and the more intense the bond, the greater the interference. The clone, by accessing dense frequencies on the subtle plane, acts as a conductor of these vibrations, retransmitting to the original emotional and psychic contents that often manifest as anxieties without apparent cause, inexplicable physical symptoms, or intrusive thoughts. The person may feel exhausted, confused, or emotionally vulnerable without understanding they are being impacted by a dissociated reflection of themselves. This phenomenon intensifies when there is vibrational correspondence, that is, when the individual continues to nurture, even unconsciously, the emotional states or mental patterns that originated the clone. The connection between them thus becomes fertile ground for maintaining repetitive cycles of suffering or stagnation, where the unresolved past gains body in the present through the active duplicate.

Understanding the nature and functioning of this bond is essential to begin the process of healing and liberation. It is not a static connection, but a flow that can be weakened, purified, or dissolved through changing the being's vibrational frequency. When the individual raises their consciousness, transforms their emotional patterns, and assumes responsibility for their energy field, the cord sustaining the clone begins to lose strength. Spiritual and therapeutic techniques—such as reconnection meditations, apometry, energetic cleansings, or reintegration rituals—are effective resources for acting on this connection, but it is the inner decision to reclaim the totality of the being that truly breaks the cycle. The energetic bond, ultimately, is a reflection of the creator's internal state. By restoring vibrational integrity and coherence between thought, emotion, and action, the being detaches from the duplicate that no longer expresses their current truth, opening space for a more lucid, centered, and sovereign presence.

It is through this bond that the clone feeds, influences, resonates in the person's body and mind. And it is through this same bond that the effects of its actions return to the creator. The energetic tie, in its essence, is ambiguous: it gives life to the clone, but also keeps it tethered. As long as this vibrational cord remains intact, the astral clone will never be a truly separate entity—it will always be acting as an extension of the host's field, silently interfering in their internal dynamics.

Many esoteric traditions speak of the existence of subtle cords between bodies: the famous silver cord, for example, connects the physical body to the astral body during conscious unfoldings or sleep. Similarly, there is a type of energetic link connecting an astral clone to its origin. This connection is not necessarily visible to everyone, but experienced mediums or trained clairvoyants can perceive it as a thread of light (in neutral or positive cases), or as a dark, thick, sometimes pulsating cord, in cases where the clone acts obsessively or parasitically.

This cord is not just a passive structure. It transports vital energy, emotions, and even mental images. When the clone is activated for some reason— whether because it was invoked, fed by recurring thoughts, or even by third-party interference—the bond intensifies. The victim immediately feels the reflections: obsessive thoughts, abrupt mood swings, energy loss, mental confusion, or even strange impulses. The clone, through this cord, sends back to the original everything it absorbs in the astral: vibrations from the environment it's in, attacks from other entities, or even the residues of its own energetic degeneration.

This phenomenon can be compared to a feedback infection. Imagine the astral clone, when exposed to vibrationally dense environments—such as regions of the umbral plane, places of spiritual suffering, or zones of obsessor activity—starts capturing these vibrations and, without an adequate barrier, retransmits them to the host. The person then begins to manifest symptoms without apparent cause: anxiety, insomnia, lethargy, lack of motivation, intrusive thoughts. In many cases, there is no external obsessing entity directly acting—what exists is the clone serving as a channel for vibrational retransmission, with the energetic bond functioning as the conductor.

This bond often forms unconsciously. When a person creates, even unintentionally, an energetic duplicate—whether through trauma, emotional repression, careless spiritual practice, or magic—the cord is automatically established as part of the connection process between creator and creature. This tie is fed by vibrational affinity: the more the person thinks or feels at the frequency that generated the clone, the stronger it becomes. And the stronger the clone, the greater its influence on the individual's state of mind, health, and decisions.

There are cases where the bond manifests through localized physical symptoms. Some people report feeling constant pressure in a specific body region—like the nape of the neck, the base of the spine, the stomach, or the chest—which has no identifiable clinical cause. In spiritual sessions, upon investigating the cause, it is discovered that the connection point of the astral clone with the victim's energy body is anchored there. On other occasions, the bond manifests in recurring dreams with a "double," an "other self" appearing trying to take control, compete, guide, or seduce. These dream experiences are not just symbolism: they are real manifestations of the exchange of impressions and interferences between the clone and the original through the energetic tie.

Breaking this bond is a crucial step in dissolving the astral clone. However, it is not a physical or mechanical cut—it is a multidimensional process involving emotional release, energetic reconfiguration, and reclaiming spiritual authority. The first move is to interrupt the energy flow sustaining the connection. This is done by changing the vibrational pattern: moving out of the frequency that originated the clone. If it was generated by fear, cultivate courage; if born of anger, develop compassion; if sustained by repressed desire, seek conscious and constructive integration of the impulse.

The second step is cleansing the connection channel. Techniques like apometry, magnetic passes, energetic baths, smudging, crystal therapy, and specific meditations can help purify the cord, weakening its capacity for interference. It is at this point that many spiritual schools apply "sealings" or "vibrational shields"—ways to prevent the clone from continuing to capture or send energy to the original. It's like placing a valve or a spiritual filter on the link connecting the two.

Then there is the definitive severance. This break does not occur by force. It is the result of a deep soul decision: to end the cycle, reintegrate the fragment, or dissolve it. In many cases, by weakening the bond, the clone loses its source of sustenance and simply dissipates. In others, an act of symbolic reintegration is necessary, where the individual welcomes what was projected and brings it back to the heart. The ritual, in this case, may involve visualizations, affirmations, astral retrievals, or shamanic practices. The key is the clear intention to close the bridge, end the duplication, and recover sovereignty over one's own field.

However, one must be vigilant: energetic bonds can try to re-establish themselves if the original emotional pattern is not transformed. That is why working with astral clones requires continuous commitment to self-knowledge, psychic hygiene, and vibrational vigilance. Breaking the bond is not an end in itself, but the beginning of a new state of presence—where the energy previously lost in duplications and fragments returns to the center, strengthening the being.

Ultimately, the energetic bond sustaining an astral clone is a reflection of the being's connection with themselves. When we are at peace, whole, conscious, and loving, there are no breaches for duplications. But when we fragment, we open space for parts of us to shift and transform into autonomous agents of interference. Awareness of this process is the first step towards its transcendence. And by breaking the bond with what no longer represents us, we open the way for reintegration with the essence—where no clone is necessary, because the inner light shines without distortions.

Chapter 15
Vital Drainage

The vital drainage caused by astral clones reveals itself as one of the most silent and, at the same time, most corrosive forms of energetic depletion a being can experience. It is a constant and invasive process, where the astral duplicate, linked to the creator's field, begins to act as a hungry extension, lacking its own energetic autonomy, feeding directly on the essential force of the one who generated it. The clone's existence depends on this continuous supply of vital energy, transforming the bond between them into an energetic outflow route, gradually compromising the person's physical, emotional, and spiritual integrity. The body begins to show signs of exhaustion, the mind becomes muddled in cognitive fogs, and the soul seems to drift away from commanding its own vehicle, creating a constant feeling of emptiness and weakening.

This phenomenon is not limited to a subjective perception of fatigue. It acts on subtle structures fundamental to sustaining life—such as chakras, meridians, and the auric field—compromising biological, psychic, and spiritual functions. Vital energy, the basis of all balance, begins to be diverted, drained by a presence that is neither external nor strange, but rather a vibrational replica created in a moment of inner rupture. Often, the individual is unaware they carry this duplicate and, therefore, seeks conventional explanations for symptoms that persist, even with rest, medication, or physical care. The clone, by remaining active, acts like a crack through which prana escapes, reducing the capacity for regeneration, emotional resilience, and spiritual connection.

In its action, the clone can act as a true saboteur of the energy system, installing itself in specific centers and draining their essential functions. This causes not only a drop in available energy but also distortion of reality perception, existential blockages, and loss of direction. The person feels demotivated, listless, unable to maintain a balanced routine or make assertive decisions. Vitality turns into weight, and the flow of life seems paralyzed. The depth of this depletion reflects the symbiotic nature of the link between clone and creator: the denser the emotional field that generated it, the more resistant and demanding the duplicate becomes. Reversing this drainage requires more than simple protection practices—it demands reclaiming inner sovereignty, consciously interrupting the energy supply to the clone, and reintegrating or definitively dissolving this extension. Only then does vital energy circulate fully again, returning lightness, clarity, and command over one's own existence to the being.

Vital energy—also called prana, chi, or etheric force, according to different traditions—is the invisible fuel sustaining not only physical health but also mental balance and emotional stability. It circulates through subtle channels, supplying chakras, organs, and structures of the energy body. When this energy is diverted or sucked by an external entity or by a semi-autonomous creation like the astral clone, the body and mind quickly collapse.

The first symptoms are subtle: constant fatigue, non-restorative sleep, difficulty concentrating, low immunity, diffuse muscle pain, a feeling of weight on the shoulders or nape, among others. In more advanced stages, vital drainage can lead to deep depression, autoimmune diseases, nervous breakdowns, and even states of dissociation. Traditional medicine usually diagnoses these symptoms as chronic stress, fatigue syndrome, depression, or anxiety, without suspecting that, behind the biochemical imbalance, an astral duplicate might be acting, silently consuming the person's energy, day after day.

The way the astral clone performs this drainage is directly proportional to its complexity and the density of the energetic bond. Simpler clones, formed by intense and momentary emotions, function like small energy vampires—sucking energy at specific moments, such as during a disturbing dream, an emotional crisis, or a vibrational dip. More complex clones, formed by old traumas or external magical manipulations, operate continuously, like open drains in the energy field. In this case, the victim feels a fatigue that doesn't pass with rest, an apathy unexplained by external factors, and a sensation of "drying out" inside, as if their willpower were being slowly emptied.

Vital drainage also directly interferes with the chakras. The solar plexus chakra, regulating self-esteem, vitality, and personal power, is usually the most affected. Clones anchoring in this center cause loss of initiative, blocks in achieving goals, and a constant feeling of inability. The heart chakra, in turn, can be hit when the clone carries affective traumas or memories of rejection. In this case, the person feels difficulty loving, maintaining healthy relationships, or even connecting with their own essence. The crown chakra, responsible for spiritual connection, can also suffer interference, especially when the clone was created to block consciousness expansion. The person begins to doubt their spirituality, feels disconnected from their faith, and enters cycles of existential emptiness.

Another important aspect of energetic drainage caused by astral clones is the impact on sleep. During rest, when the physical body is disconnected from conscious functions, the energy field expands, and the astral body naturally projects. It is at this moment that the astral clone becomes more active. It can take part of the projected astral body's energy, leading it to dense vibrational regions, causing agitated dreams, sleep paralysis, sensations of falling or persecution. When the individual returns to the physical body, instead of feeling refreshed, they wake up even more tired, with pain, a feeling of heaviness, and sometimes memory lapses or mild psychic disturbances.

In extreme situations, vital drainage can open space for more severe spiritual illnesses. The weakening of the energy field makes the individual vulnerable to astral larvae, obsessors, and other parasitic entities. The clone, by sucking energy, creates actual "cracks" in the aura, through which other beings take advantage to install themselves. This explains why many cases of spiritual possession or deep obsession are associated with the prior existence of an active astral clone, functioning as an entry point for vibrational infestation.

Reversing this situation begins with identifying the problem. Recognizing that there is abnormal energetic drainage is the first step. Spiritual sensitivity techniques—such as aura reading, radiesthesia, apometry, or even energetic scanning by mediums—help locate the source of the leak. Once the astral clone is identified as the draining agent, a process of detachment and purification must begin. This may involve various approaches: baths with herbs like rue, rosemary, and guinea-hen weed; smudging with white sage, myrrh incense, or specific resins; sessions of energetic passes, Reiki, chakra alignment, and apometric deprogramming commands.

However, the clone's dissolution will only be effective if accompanied by the victim's internal transformation. This is because the clone feeds not only on vital energy but also on the emotional patterns that keep it alive. If the person continues vibrating in fear, anger, guilt, or desire for escape, they will continue nourishing the clone, even after cleansing rituals. It is necessary to reclaim will, strengthen self-esteem, cultivate elevated thoughts, and, above all, retake command of one's own life. The presence of a clone indicates that something within the being was left adrift.

And healing involves rescuing this internal territory, sealing its borders, and reaffirming the soul's sovereignty over its own energy.

Furthermore, it is essential to create a vibrational environment favoring energetic regeneration. This involves simple daily practices, like sleeping in a clean, airy, and spiritually protected room (with crystals, mantras, prayers, or protection symbols); avoiding excessive consumption of negative content (news, horror movies, low-frequency music); cultivating healthy relationships, and practicing inner silence. Vital energy is not just a resource—it reflects the harmony between body, mind, and spirit. When the being is aligned, energy circulates freely. When there is rupture, the flow is interrupted, and leaks appear.

It is important to remember that no astral clone sustains itself without permission—even if unconscious. The energetic cord feeding this entity mirrors the individual's own disconnection from their essence. By re-establishing this connection, by turning inward with honesty and love, the natural energy flow is restored. The clone then loses strength, dissolves, or is reintegrated, and vitality returns with renewed force. Fatigue gives way to lightness. Apathy transforms into motivation. And the soul, finally, fully inhabits the body again, without shares, shadows, or duplicates. Only itself—whole, alive, and free.

Chapter 16
Mental Influence

In the scenario of interactions between subtle planes and human consciousness, the mental field emerges as a territory vulnerable to influences operating beyond ordinary perception. Among these hidden forces, the astral clone stands out as a psychic agent endowed with the ability to mimic individuality, deeply interfering with the being's mental and emotional integrity. Acting from the astral plane, this energetic duplicate not only reflects aspects of the individual but also manipulates them, distorting thoughts, emotions, and perceptions in a manner as subtle as it is penetrating. Its power of influence is not limited to suggestions or fleeting inspirations but reaches a level of symbiosis with the person's psychic field, shaping their mental states with almost surgical precision.

This form of interference establishes itself through a vibrational link allowing the clone to access and alter the internal flows of the original mind. It inserts itself into the invisible webs where memories, desires, fears, and beliefs intertwine, becoming an almost undetectable but intensely operative presence. Unlike external forces attempting to influence from the outside in, the astral clone infiltrates the core of the psyche, disguising itself as legitimate thought, spontaneous feeling, or revealing insight. The mind, under this influence, begins exhibiting paradoxical behaviors, emotional oscillations without apparent cause, and a constant sense of internal misalignment, as if something were displaced or artificial in the way of thinking and feeling.

This influence intensifies in moments when consciousness drifts from active vigilance, such as during states of fatigue, stress, melancholy, or excessive mental stimulation. In these moments, the clone exploits vibrational fragility to sow contents that confuse and obscure discernment. The astral clone's action, therefore, is silent, persistent, and strategic, often going unnoticed by those lacking a constant practice of self-observation and mental hygiene. Understanding its existence and recognizing its manifestation signs is a crucial step towards regaining command of one's own mind and restoring internal balance, as only with consciousness is it possible to neutralize a presence that feeds on inattention and self-ignorance.

It is necessary to understand that the human mental field is not limited to logical and rational thought. It is a set of interactive layers involving beliefs, memories, archetypes, impulses, and, above all, vibrational frequencies. The mind is a space where different voices compete for the primacy of consciousness, and it is in this silent theater that the astral clone acts masterfully. Being connected to the person's psychic field, the clone becomes a transmitter and amplifier of mental contents, many of them disharmonious. Its existence creates an internal echo—a duplication of will that, although seeming to originate from the individual themselves, is actually the result of the double's action.

The first perceptible symptom of this influence is the intensification of negative thought patterns. What was once just a timid doubt transforms into a paralyzing conviction. A common insecurity grows and converts into chronic fear. A past grievance magnifies, becoming an acidic resentment consuming the present's emotional energy. The astral clone, in this scenario, acts like a distorting lens amplifying the darkest aspects within the human psyche. It resonates with frequencies of pain, guilt, fear, and anger, replicating these feelings in waves, until the individual finds themselves dominated by emotions they don't fully comprehend.

Being anchored in the mental plane, the clone has direct access to the person's thoughts. And more than that: it can generate thoughts. This is one of the most alarming facets of mental influence exerted by astral clones. Unlike an external obsessor, who insinuates ideas through vibrational approximation, the astral clone emits thoughts from the inside out, as if native to the victim's mind. The difference between authentic thought and induced thought then becomes almost impossible to perceive. The person begins hearing, within themselves, voices subtly different from their usual consciousness—sometimes depreciative, sometimes seductive, but invariably deviant from their original axis.

This mechanism is widely reported in therapeutic and spiritualist sessions. Individuals claiming to have intrusive thoughts—of self-destruction, violence, abandonment, or escape—are often surprised to discover such ideas did not arise spontaneously but were reinforced by the continuous action of an astral clone. In some cases, these thoughts are accompanied by vivid, almost hallucinatory mental images, appearing during moments of emotional vulnerability, like sleep, meditation, or altered states of consciousness. The clone, in this action, not only whispers but paints entire mental scenarios, creating parallel realities where the person sees themselves in situations of defeat, humiliation, or helplessness.

Another notable effect is the temporary alteration of personality traits. People who are normally calm and peaceful might exhibit disproportionate bursts of anger. Gentle and loving individuals might suddenly become cold, cynical, or manipulative. These episodes don't sustain over time but leave a trail of guilt and perplexity, as the person, upon regaining control, feels as if "possessed" by a distorted version of themselves. And, in a way, they were. The astral clone, by taking command of emitting certain thoughts, can modulate emotional and behavioral states very effectively, especially when finding a conducive vibrational field—that is, when the victim is energetically low.

This interference can reach extreme levels. There are reports of people who, under the influence of astral clones, began doubting their sanity. The clone acts like an internal shadow constantly questioning decisions, sabotaging initiatives, and distorting memories. The victim starts feeling they can no longer trust their own feelings, as if spied on from within. This type of fragmentation of psychic trust is one of the most severe forms of mental influence, as it shakes the foundations of the self. The mind, which should be the bastion of autonomy and discernment, becomes a battlefield where the original and the clone dispute command over ideas.

In more complex contexts, especially when the clone was programmed by third parties (as in cases of negative magic or sophisticated obsession), it can be instructed to insert specific ideas into the victim's mind. For example, it might induce isolation, suggesting everyone around is hostile. It might create a compulsion for self-destructive behaviors, like addictions, extreme procrastination, sabotaging relationships, or abandoning important opportunities. The mind then transforms into a labyrinth where every exit seems to lead back to the starting point, perpetuating the cycle of suffering.

However, the astral clone is not limited to reinforcing negative aspects. In some situations, it simulates positive thoughts, intending to create illusory distractions. The individual begins deceiving themselves, believing they are evolving spiritually, when, in fact, they are being led away from their true purpose. It's the illusion of enlightenment—one of the most sophisticated tricks of the lower astral plane. The clone, in this case, praises, caresses, inflames the ego, making the person feel special artificially, preventing them from recognizing their real growth needs. This masked action is common in people dealing with spirituality superficially or thirsting for power without ethical preparation.

Identifying the mental action of an astral clone requires keen inner listening and constant self-observation. The first warning sign is the emergence of recurring thoughts dissonant with the individual's usual pattern. Secondly, thoughts arising with disproportionate emotional intensity should be observed: if an idea is accompanied by a surge of intense anger, fear, or sadness, it might not be just one's own thought. It is also important to note if there are marked internal contradictions—like desiring something and then having an automatic impulse to sabotage that desire.

The liberation process from this influence begins with recognition: understanding that not everything we think is genuinely ours. This simple realization already starts deactivating the clone's power. Next, re-establishing the mental command center is necessary, through practices like meditation, conscious affirmations, prayer, journaling (reflective writing), and, when necessary, specific spiritual interventions. The practice of mindfulness—being present in the now—is a powerful tool, as it prevents the clone from acting on the automatisms of the unconscious mind.

Another fundamental step is reclaiming will. The clone exploits moments when the person's will is weakened, confused, or dormant. Strengthening the ability to choose, to say "yes" and "no" clearly, to commit to oneself, is the path to reassuming the throne of one's own consciousness. In many esoteric traditions, will is the soul's power point—and strengthening it is like reigniting the inner sun that dispels shadows.

It is also important to cleanse the mental field of vibrational residues. Thoughts have form and, over time, form psychic clouds around the person. When these clouds are dense, the clone finds a fertile environment to manifest. Techniques like visualizing violet light over the mind, cleansing mantras, and using sacred symbols act as neutralizers of these mental miasmas. The goal is to restore the mind's original frequency, returning its clarity, peace, and discernment.

The astral clone, when deprived of the possibility of mental influence, loses much of its power. Therefore, rather than trying to destroy it directly, it is often more effective to remove its stage. By recognizing one's own mind as a sacred temple and making it impassable to strange voices, the being shields itself against the silent invasion of the double. And, over time, what seemed like an internal adversary reveals itself merely as an echo that no longer finds resonance. The mind calms. The will firms up. The essence retakes command. And the clone, silenced by lack of sustenance, dissolves like a forgotten dream at dawn.

Chapter 17
Astral Parasite

In the denser regions of the astral plane, subtle life forms arise that not only coexist with human energy but consume it as a means of survival, establishing distorted symbiotic connections with their victims' energy fields. These entities, originating from the degeneration of psychic constructs created by the individual themselves, transcend the original function of vibrational duplicates and assume a destructive and autonomous role. An astral clone, when completely losing its attunement with the energetic matrix that originated it, acquires characteristics approaching a rudimentary and predatory consciousness. It ceases to be just a deformed extension of someone's emotional or mental identity and begins operating as an astral parasite: an entity anchoring itself in the subtle field and feeding directly on the person's vitality, causing profound imbalances on different levels of the being.

This transformation process does not occur abruptly, but through a series of vibrational events making the clone progressively denser, more resistant to natural dissolution, and less influenceable by the creator's consciousness. Over time, it develops an almost animal instinct, guided solely by the search for energetic sustenance. From this phase, the clone not only reproduces negative emotional patterns but intensifies, re-feeds, and perpetuates them, seeking fragile points in the host's energy field to attach itself more efficiently. Its presence tends to be subtle initially, masked by common daily symptoms, but accentuates as it finds breaches in the individual's emotional, spiritual, or mental state, infiltrating like a constant and silent presence, but with cumulative effect.

The astral parasite, originating from this vibrational mutation, is a master of camouflage and manipulation, operating with the instinctive intelligence typical of simpler life forms, yet with great effectiveness in the subtle world. It knows the host's vibrations because it was born from them; understands emotional frailties because it fed on them; exploits psychic breaches because they were its cradle. Its action does not aim at evil itself, but the perpetuation of its existence, making it especially dangerous, as it acts without guilt, morality, or remorse, operating exclusively based on energetic survival. By understanding this dynamic, it becomes possible to unveil the signs of its presence, not as random external manifestations, but as internal alerts that something created by the psyche itself has gotten out of control and begun exerting dominance over the personal energy field. This recognition marks the beginning of the liberation process, requiring not only energetic cleansing but, above all, profound work of reintegration and inner healing.

The transition from clone to parasite is not sudden, but gradual. Initially, the clone still maintains some degree of attunement with its generator, orbiting specific emotions, recurring thoughts, or repressed desires. However, over time—and especially in the absence of spiritual and emotional vigilance—it densifies, solidifies, autonomizes, and breaks identity ties. It becomes something distinct, though connected, and this "something" is thirsty. The vital energy that once flowed spontaneously for life maintenance is now captured by invisible tentacles attached to the dark double.

Unlike external spiritual entities, like obsessors or disturbing spirits, the parasitic clone has the advantage—or rather, the trap—of carrying the victim's same vibrational signature. This makes its identification harder and its influence more effective. It camouflages itself within the aura, adapts to emotional field oscillations, responds to mental impulses as if part of the original system. But in its essence, it is no longer a distorted "self." It is a "non-self" parasitizing the being, strengthening with each emotional collapse, each thought of guilt, each act of self-sabotage.

The typical behavior of an astral parasite created from a clone is characterized by cycles of intensification and retreat. In certain periods, the victim feels relatively well, as if the problem had disappeared. At other times, especially after emotionally draining experiences, the parasite manifests strongly: sudden exhaustion, causeless discouragement, creative blocks, memory loss, apathy, a feeling of weight on the shoulders, medically unexplained pain, and thoughts sabotaging any attempt at spiritual or material progress.

One of the favorite attachment regions for these parasites is the solar plexus—the energy center responsible for personal identity, will, and action in the world. When a parasitic clone anchors there, it is common for the individual to experience loss of self-esteem, feelings of devaluation, and a persistent belief they are incapable or undeserving. The feeding occurs through continuous draining of energies of realization and enthusiasm, creating a kind of "vacuum" in the soul, where dreams seem distant and the joy of living becomes pale.

Another frequent attack point is the heart chakra. When the parasite connects in this region, it interferes with the deepest emotions, especially self-love and the capacity for connection with others. The victim may begin feeling unworthy of affection, plunge into solitude, or develop an irrational fear of abandonment. Affective relationships become fragile, often contaminated by jealousy, distrust, or affective blocks inconsistent with reality but fed by the emotional field manipulated by the parasitic presence.

The astral parasite derived from a clone can also act in the mental field, generating noise and thought distortions. It stimulates rumination, excessive self-criticism, pathological perfectionism, and, in more advanced cases, leads to mental paralysis. The mind enters a cycle of circular ideas, where there is no logical or emotional exit—only repetition. The being thinks, rethinks, sinks into doubts, and, in the end, does not act.

The paralysis of will is the parasite's objective, as it is in this state that it feeds most easily, sucking the energy contained in frustrations and unfulfilled desires.

Importantly, the parasitic astral clone can have multiple energetic "mouths": attachment points distributed throughout the aura and subtle bodies. In certain cases, the person's field resembles a network of connections where each point is being sucked by a part of the fragmented clone. The individual begins living a kind of constant energy leak, with symptoms alternating between physical, emotional, and mental, making spiritual diagnosis even more challenging.

The presence of an astral parasite generated from a clone can also cause alterations in sleep cycles. The individual may report recurring dreams of persecution, visions of dark doubles, sensations of suffocation, or feeling their body pulled by something invisible during sleep. They might wake up mid-night with tachycardia, cold sweats, feeling something observed or touched them. These phenomena indicate the parasite acts more intensely during the natural unfolding of sleep, when ego defense mechanisms are relaxed and the person's astral field is more exposed.

From an esoteric viewpoint, this type of parasite possesses limited intelligence but vibrational cunning. It knows how to maintain itself, what it needs to survive, and where to hide in the host's field. It is not a malignant entity in the traditional sense, as it lacks an agenda of malice—its sole motivation is survival. But this makes it even more dangerous, as it will act incessantly to ensure its permanence, even if it costs the psychic, emotional, or even physical life of its host.

Combating this type of parasite requires an integral approach. The first measure is identification. Techniques like mediumistic scanning, energy reading with crystals, use of radiesthesia, or apometry sessions are effective in locating attachment points. Once identified, the cleansing process must begin. Spiritual cleansings with herbs, crystals, discharge baths, and smudging are effective in dislodging the entity from anchor points. Magnetic passes, Reiki application, specific prayers, and apometric commands are important resources in the vibrational extraction process of the parasite.

However, no external cleaning will be lasting if the person's vibrational field is not readjusted internally. The parasite only finds dwelling where there is resonance with pain, fear, hatred, guilt, and denial. Therefore, the healing process necessarily involves a dive into self-knowledge. Regressive therapies, family constellations, psychotherapy, deep meditations, and forgiveness practices are valuable tools for healing the wounds feeding the parasite. The goal is to eliminate the "vibrational foods" sustaining it, cutting off its energy source.

Furthermore, sealing the energy fields is necessary, preventing the entity's reinsertion or the formation of new parasitic clones. Energetic shielding techniques with visualizations, creating fields of light, using mantras and sacred symbols, as well as consecrating personal amulets, help keep the aura intact and inaccessible. Maintaining high vibration through regular spiritual practices, gratitude, contact with nature, and good energetic nutrition (including music, readings, and healthy coexistence) completes the protection process.

It is fundamental to remember that every astral parasite is also a mirror of something unlooked at. It forms from what was repressed, rejected, or ignored within the psyche itself. Instead of just expelling, one must understand. The true exorcism is the light of consciousness. When we become whole, what is fragmented finds nowhere to attach. When we love ourselves deeply, what is shadow finds no breach to act. And when we align with our innermost truth, what is dissonant simply does not resonate. The parasitic astral clone is, then, an extreme opportunity to awaken. It brutally shows where we are disconnected from our essence. It is up to each individual to look at this part of themselves—or their history—with courage, compassion, and a sincere desire for healing. For only then, by illuminating what was created in shadow, does true freedom establish itself. And the being returns to their center, free of parasites, complete in themselves, absolute master of their own light.

Chapter 18
Physical Signs

The interaction between the physical body and the subtler energy fields reveals a profound and sensitive intelligence, where each vibrational disturbance reflects as an organic signal, often ignored by the rational mind. When an astral clone reaches the parasitic stage, its action is not limited to the invisible domains—it infiltrates the bodily structure and directly interferes with the organism's vitality. The body, perceiving this interference, begins emitting alerts in the form of symptoms challenging traditional medical logic. Such signs are not isolated manifestations but integrated responses to a broader reality, in which the human being is both matter and energy, body and spirit.

By acting on the vital field, the astral clone unbalances the flow of essential force, creating breaches through which continuous physical depletion sets in. This depletion does not occur uniformly or superficially; it manifests with specific characteristics denouncing the extraphysical origin of the problem. The body begins operating in a state of permanent compensation, trying to balance the deficits created by the clone's draining action. In this attempt at self-regulation, persistent symptoms arise such as unexplained fatigue, metabolic disorders, sleep rhythm alterations, and a series of discomforts conventional clinical exams cannot explain. The subtle field, overloaded, impacts bodily systems—especially those most sensitive to energy, like the nervous, endocrine, and immune systems—making the individual more vulnerable to illnesses and states of mental confusion.

Physical signs are, therefore, the final layer of a process beginning on the higher planes of existence, where the clone's influence acts almost imperceptibly, but devastatingly long-term. By recognizing these symptoms do not arise by chance, but as expressions of an intelligent and persistent energetic interference, the possibility of true healing expands. The body is not just a passive victim of these forces, but an ally communicating, warning, and guiding. Each unexplained pain, each sensation of weight, each inexplicable alteration in the organism's natural cycles is an invitation to self-knowledge and spiritual investigation. Facing these signs as symbolic language—and not just as disorders to be suppressed—allows access to the deep causes of imbalance, opening the way for integral restoration beyond symptom relief. Thus, understanding the physical signs of an astral clone's presence is, above all, an exercise in inner listening, of subtly reading one's own bodily temple, crying out for reconnection with its original source of light and vitality.

The first sign, and perhaps the most common, is chronic fatigue. This tiredness does not yield to rest. Even after long nights of sleep, the person awakens feeling more exhausted than when they went to bed. It's as if something drained their life force during the night—and indeed, that's exactly what happens. The clone's action, especially while consciousness is unfolded in sleep, intensifies its energetic feeding, using the original's energy to stay active. The body, in turn, without receiving the natural energetic replenishment from rest, begins operating at a deficit, generating a state of permanent exhaustion.

Another recurrent manifestation is unexplained weight changes. Some people report accelerated weight loss without changing diet or physical routine, while others gain weight even with controlled eating. These extremes indicate imbalances in the body's energy metabolism, resulting from the clone's interference. The endocrine system, regulating glands and hormones, is particularly sensitive to the action of disharmonious subtle fields. When constantly bombarded by distorted frequencies originating from a parasitic double, it malfunctions, causing chain reactions expressed in abrupt gain or loss of body mass.

Sudden pallor, deep dark circles under the eyes, and an appearance of physical wear are other visible signs. The astral clone, by sucking vital energy, compromises prana flow—the subtle energy field permeating bodily systems. The skin loses its glow, eyes seem dull, and there's a general loss of physical tone. Even in young people, one can observe an aged or worn-out countenance, as if something were consuming them from within. It's as if the clone's shadow projected onto the face, giving it an opaque appearance, devoid of the vital spark.

Localized sensations in the body are also frequent. Many report pain or heaviness in the nape and shoulders, indicating energetic overload or parasitic presence in that region. The crown center (top of the head) and the medulla chakra (base of the skull) are access points used by astral entities to insert commands or establish vibrational connections. When the clone acts there, it's common for the person to experience recurrent headaches, ringing in the ears, or pressure on the forehead. Others describe a constant coldness in a specific body part, usually associated with where the clone anchored part of its presence.

In some situations, symptoms similar to physical illnesses arise but are not confirmed by clinical exams. The person might present palpitations, sweating, tingling in limbs, dizziness, and even panic attack symptoms, without any identifiable medical origin. These episodes are usually preceded or followed by vivid dreams of persecution, dark environments, or encounters with threatening figures. These dreams are not just products of imagination: they are astral memories of interactions with the clone or associated entities.

Interference with sleep, incidentally, is one of the most direct physical signs of an astral clone's action. The person might suffer from inexplicable insomnia, waking up several times during the night for no apparent reason. Or they might feel as if being pulled from the body, waking with startles or a falling sensation. In more advanced stages of parasitism, cases of sleep paralysis are reported—a condition where the mind awakens, but the body remains immobile, often accompanied by a feeling of presence in the room. In these moments, the clone approaches or even tries to reassume dominance over the victim's energy field.

More intense cases include manifestations visible to third parties. Stories of involuntary bilocation—when someone is seen in two places at once—are ancient and documented accounts. One of the most famous is that of the French teacher Émilie Sagée, who, in the mid-19th century, was frequently seen in duplicate by her students and colleagues. While teaching in the classroom, an exact copy of her would appear performing the same gestures or standing silently in another corner of the room. After such events, Émilie became extremely debilitated, as if her vitality had been drained by the active clone. This type of phenomenon, although rare, precisely illustrates how the clone can acquire enough autonomy to partially interact with the physical world.

Skin sensitivity can also be altered. Some report causeless itching, a sensation of something crawling under the skin, tingling, or constant chills in certain body regions, even in warm environments. These signs are interpreted by many spiritual therapists as manifestations of the etheric presence of a being installed in the bioenergetic field. The clone, being a form highly attuned to the host's own vibration, doesn't need much to provoke tactile sensations—a mere emotional oscillation or negative thought is enough for its action to intensify.

The immune system also suffers from energetic drainage. A person under the influence of a parasitic clone might get sick more often, have difficulty recovering, or develop low immunity conditions even without prior clinical history. The body, deprived of the spiritual vitality that normally reinforces its defense, becomes vulnerable to physical invaders. It's the materialization of the esoteric principle that all imbalance begins on subtle planes and only later manifests in the physical body.

Not infrequently, the clone can manifest in external phenomena related to the body. Mirrors darkening in its presence, reflections seemingly moving with delay, shadows appearing in peripheral vision, strange noises coming from the room during the night—these are events frequently reported by those living with advanced astral clones. These phenomena are not isolated delusions or hallucinations, but signs that the clone's action is reaching the threshold between subtle and dense.

When the physical body begins clearly manifesting the clone's influence, it's a sign the astral process is already at an advanced stage. This demands urgent and integral intervention. Seeking mere physical relief will not suffice—it's necessary to go to the spiritual root of the problem. Physical symptoms are just reflections of a deeper battle fought on the energetic plane, and only by winning this combat can the body regenerate.

Ancient wisdom already affirmed the body is the spirit's temple. And as such, it reacts to any strange presence wanting to install itself without permission. Pain, exhaustion, disorders are the bells of this temple, warning there's an invader, a maladjustment, a presence that doesn't belong. Listening attentively to these bells is the first step to regaining sovereignty over body and soul. And once the invisible cause is identified, the process of purification and liberation can begin, restoring health as a natural expression of inner harmony.

Chapter 19
Psychic Signs

The psychic domain, by its very invisible and subjective nature, becomes the most vulnerable field to the subtle action of parasitic intelligences like astral clones. There is no resistance more fragile than that which believes itself protected by the familiarity of its own thoughts. When an astral clone inserts itself into this territory, it does so with disguised mastery, using the original consciousness's vibrational signature to manipulate the mind from within. The process is not perceived as invasion, but as internal disarray, as if something were "wrong" with the person themselves—a thought, incidentally, reinforced by the clone itself as a strategy to undermine the host's confidence and sense of identity. It is in this scenario that psychic signs emerge, not as external flashes of disturbance, but as subtle alterations in the person's mental, emotional, and perceptual flow, intensifying as the parasitic presence consolidates.

Initially, alterations might manifest as mild mental confusion, concentration lapses, and loss of clarity in daily tasks. These signs, when recurrent and without practical explanation, already indicate the psychic energy flow is being intercepted. As the clone's action advances, self-deprecating thoughts, feelings of inadequacy, unjustified fear, and episodes of deep anguish without direct cause arise. These mental contents are not created by the individual but reactivated and amplified by the clone's vibrational frequency, acting as a catalyst for everything repressed, unresolved, or imbalanced within the psychic field. The feeling that there's an "internal presence" influencing decisions, attitudes, or emotions is an important alert, though often ignored for fear of seeming irrational. However, it is precisely at this point the clone acts most: in the mind's blind spot, where doubt and fear intertwine with the illusion of control.

As the clone strengthens, the emotional structure begins showing evident instability. Mood swings without concrete justification, difficulty maintaining high vibrational states, a sense of detachment from one's own essence, and loss of the ability to truly feel emotions are indications the soul is gradually being encapsulated in a psychic veil of interference. This veil prevents consciousness expansion and connection with higher dimensions of being, isolating the individual in dense and repetitive mental patterns. Thoughts become circular, always returning to the same fears, frustrations, and insecurities. At this point, the clone not only influences but occupies the space of will, hindering conscious choices and blocking transformative initiatives. The being, then, does not just think what they feel—they feel what the clone induces them to think. And this silent inversion is one of the most dangerous signs of psychic domination. The only way out is to break this cycle with awakened consciousness, reactivating inner sovereignty and reintegrating the parts of the mind hijacked by this presence disguised as familiarity.

The psychic signs that an astral clone is active and interfering in someone's mind do not follow Cartesian logic. They reveal themselves as pattern breaks, ruptures in habitual behavior, fissures in self-perception. One of the subtlest, yet most severe, manifestations is the feeling of otherness: the individual feels, at certain moments, that there is "someone else" inside them. This is not a literal hallucination, but a faint perception that thoughts and feelings arise autonomously, as if whispered by a parallel consciousness. This type of experience is often ignored or rationalized but represents one of the clearest signs that a second center of will is operating in sync with the original.

Besides this feeling of otherness, there are intrusive thoughts. These manifest as sudden ideas, often violent, depressive, or self-deprecating, arising without apparent cause and inconsistent with the person's emotional profile. A calm individual might be seized by inexplicable bursts of anger; an optimistic person might plunge into deep melancholy out of nowhere; a loving person might suddenly feel hatred for loved ones. Such impulses are not the result of a mental disorder in the clinical sense, but rather the vibrational reflection of the astral clone's action, projecting onto the victim's mind the energetic patterns from which it was created.

The clone, especially when originating from repressed emotions or unresolved traumas, carries a frequency that magnetizes similar experiences. It attracts thoughts and emotions congruent with its nature. Thus, if generated from fear, it continuously instigates mental situations of insecurity, phobias, or catastrophism. If emerged from repressed anger, it pushes the individual towards states of passive aggression, resentment, and explosive behavior. The most dangerous aspect is that, since these emotions were already latent in the host's psyche, their expression occurs "naturally," making it difficult to perceive an external agent acting behind the repetition of these patterns.

Dreams also suffer direct interference from the astral clone. Generally, reports point to dreams with repetitive content, dark scenarios, threatening presences, or distorted versions of the dreamer themselves. A common motif in these dreams is encountering a "dark twin"—a copy of the individual pursuing, challenging, or observing them with a judgmental gaze. In other cases, the clone manifests as a figure assuming the dreamer's form and acting in their place, often making wrong or harmful decisions. What many don't understand is that these dreams are not merely symbolic: they represent the clone's real activity during sleep, a time when the psychic defense field is naturally more open.

Another powerful indicator of an astral clone's presence is the growing difficulty in maintaining positive and constructive thoughts. The mind seems hijacked by a fog of negativity, making the exercise of prayer, concentration, and meditation arduous. The victim tries to elevate spiritually but soon feels dispersed, tired, or overcome by doubts. This occurs because the clone acts directly on the higher psychic centers, trying to prevent consciousness from accessing higher vibrational states. The higher the thought, the more it threatens the clone's existence, which depends on dense frequencies to continue existing.

Emotional instability, with abrupt mood swings, is another evident sign. In a single day, the person might oscillate between euphoria and sadness, hope and despair, enthusiasm and lethargy. These fluctuations are unrelated to concrete events and are, most often, misunderstood even by those affected. Those living with such individuals frequently notice these changes as "strange" or "unusual" behaviors, generating conflicts and social isolation. Isolation, incidentally, is a direct consequence of the clone's action, feeding on the host's emotional disconnection and weakening affective bonds.

Memory can also be affected. Small lapses, frequent forgetfulness, confusion of dates, or even temporary loss of time sense are common. In more severe cases, reports of dissociative episodes arise, where the person performs actions they later don't clearly remember. This is not medical amnesia, but moments when the clone partially assumes control of decisions or directly interferes with reality perception. These memory breaches are dangerous, indicating progressive erosion of the person's psychic sovereignty over their own mind.

Intuition is also negatively affected. People who previously had sharp sensitivity to perceive environments, capture vibrations, or receive insights start feeling "disconnected" or "unplugged." This desensitization is not natural—it's caused by the clone's field, interfering with higher channels of subtle perception. As a result, the victim loses the ability to perceive energetic dangers, becomes more susceptible to spiritual traps, and distances themselves from connections with their mentors or spiritual guides. In other words, the clone creates an inverse shield: instead of protecting, it isolates, silences, and obscures the inner light.

Often, the affected person develops an internal vocabulary of self-sabotage. Phrases like "I'm not capable," "I won't succeed," "Everything goes wrong for me" become part of the daily mental repertoire. This type of internal discourse, though seemingly just psychological, is frequently induced vibrationally by the clone. It echoes these phrases in the host's mind, feeding a cycle of impotence and devaluation preventing them from reacting. It's as if the clone itself, by installing itself as an inner voice, were molding a new negative personality, overlaying the person's true essence.

Perhaps the subtlest and most devastating psychic sign is the gradual emptying of life's meaning. The person no longer feels pleasure in activities that once brought joy. Enthusiasm disappears, projects lose importance, and existence seems reduced to a gray automatism. This state of deep apathy, often confused with depression, indicates the clone has been in control for a long time, draining not only energy but also the soul's purpose. The being enters a mode of psychic survival, merely fulfilling routines but not truly living.

Recognizing these signs is essential. They should not be ignored or treated solely with medication or conventional therapies, although these can be useful supports. The key lies in understanding that behind these mental and emotional manifestations, a subtle entity is acting—an entity needing detection, confrontation, and dissolution with consciousness, will, and light. For the mind, like the body and spirit, is a sacred temple. And no invader, however much disguised as part of the self, can remain where there is clarity, firmness, and truth.

Chapter 20
Spiritual Detection

Recognizing subtle presences influencing personal reality demands a specific type of perception: one transcending common senses and anchoring in listening to the invisible. Detecting an astral clone, especially when lodged deeply and silently in someone's energy field, requires activating spiritual faculties capable of perceiving what cannot be touched, but which nevertheless leaves clear marks on daily life. The process does not begin, as many imagine, with an external diagnosis. Before that, it arises as internal discomfort, an insistent intuition that something is out of order—not in the external world, but in the intimate landscape of one's own existence. This subtle unease, almost always rationalized or dismissed, is actually one of the first signs the soul perceives the imbalance, even when the mind still tries to deny it.

Spiritual investigation thus becomes an indispensable instrument for anyone seeking to understand the invisible causes of their blockages, pains, or repetitive emotional states. Unlike traditional therapeutic approaches working with symptoms, spiritual investigation delves into the vibrational root of the problem. It requires surrender, listening, and willingness to face what was projected to remain hidden. Often, the astral clone does not present itself as a clear or threatening entity. It hides under the guise of personality itself, disguised as habits, emotional patterns, automatic reactions. This camouflage hinders its identification by common methods. However, as spiritual perception deepens, images, sensations, and messages emerge revealing the double's presence—whether through recurring dreams, identity lapses, or symbolic visions during altered states of consciousness.

The trained spiritual gaze, like that of mediums, energy therapists, or workers of specific spiritual lines, can function as an amplified mirror of the soul. These professionals capture, through different techniques and sensitivities, condensed thought-forms, zones of vibrational stagnation, distortions in the auric field, and presences linked by invisible cords to the person's energy. However, even before seeking external help, the person themselves can become an investigator of themselves. Self-knowledge, allied with the practice of meditation, conscious prayer, and regular energetic cleansing, begins opening the internal curtains where the clone usually operates. Perception starts changing. What was once just fatigue, sadness, or anxiety, begins being understood as interference. What was once confused with personality traits reveals itself as subtle impositions of an "other self." This recognition is transformative, initiating a new cycle: that of conscious responsibility over one's own light, shadow, and everything inhabiting the space between them.

For many, the first step towards detection is self-observation. The individual, feeling the previously described physical and psychic signs, begins intuiting something in their life is influenced by a force not entirely their own. At this point, intuition plays a valuable role: it whispers there's a foreign element, something "out of place" in their daily experience. This suspicion is the starting point. However, confirming it's an astral clone requires more refined instruments, capable of probing the hidden layers of being.

Mediums (clairvoyant, sensitive) and spiritual therapists are the first allies on this journey. Clairvoyance is the faculty of seeing beyond the physical world—and it's precisely through it that many astral clones are perceived. In energetic sessions, like those conducted in spiritualist centers, apometry houses, or esoteric clinics, the experienced medium can identify the presence of a subtle form attached to the person's field. This form often appears as a silhouette of the querent themselves, glued to their aura or positioned just behind the physical body. The medium, describing this image, often speaks of a "doppelgänger," a "double," or a "shadow with human form" accompanying the patient. Such reports, though symbolic, accurately reflect the astral clone's presence.

Other professionals use specific techniques for this detection. Radiesthesia, for example, is widely employed. Using pendulums or aurameters, the therapist checks the individual's vibrational field, detecting zones of blockage, imbalance, or energetic overlap. When an active astral clone is present, the pendulum tends to oscillate irregularly or indicate an anomalous energetic polarity. In some cases, it's even possible to map the clone's location in the person's auric field: over the head, on the back, to the left or right side, depending on how its formation and attachment occurred.

Kirlian photography, although still considered controversial academically, is another tool used by spiritual therapists. This technique captures the body's energetic radiation and, on some occasions, reveals unusual light patterns around the subject, as if there were duplications or shadows attached to the main aura. Some records show a second, fainter silhouette superimposed on the individual's body. These visual signs, interpreted by specialists, can indicate the presence of a duplicated form, astral in origin.

In the realm of dreams and consciousness projection, astral clone detection takes on even more fascinating contours. Individuals practicing conscious astral unfolding, i.e., able to leave the physical body during sleep or through meditative techniques, sometimes encounter their own image at a distance. This vision is neither metaphor nor hallucination: it is, most likely, encountering one's own clone. Some describe these experiences with astonishment: seeing a figure identical to themselves, but acting strangely, walking through dark places, or observing them coldly. These encounters are revealing. The awakened practitioner recognizes there's another "self" acting autonomously, indicating a part of their psychic energy unfolded and gained its own life.

Specialized spiritualist groups, like those practicing apometry, offer more structured approaches for detecting astral clones. Apometry is a technique combining magnetic passes, rhythmic counting, and mental command to unfold subtle bodies and directly access spiritual planes. In an apometry session, mediums project themselves to investigate the patient's energy field under the guidance of spiritual mentors. In these investigations, clones are frequently located hidden in dense astral sub-planes, encased in containment fields, or coupled to the querent's psychosphere like true parasitic modules. Reports from mediums describe these forms with surprising detail: some are completely similar to the patient, while others are distorted, with features of suffering, anger, or sadness—reflecting the type of energy that gave rise to them.

It's important to highlight that, sometimes, the astral clone doesn't appear as a complete figure. In many cases, it's identified as a fragment of the patient's own soul, a traumatized emotional part that detached and began acting as a semi-independent entity. These forms, seen by mediums or perceived by sensitives, are described as "wounded inner children," "weeping doubles," or "fragments of pain." Their detection requires emotional sensitivity and spiritual communication ability, as often these fragments need welcoming, understanding, and reintegration into the whole consciousness, rather than simple banishment.

Some people, even without developed mediumistic gifts, report clearly perceiving the clone's presence. They feel it as a shadow accompanying them, a voice not their own, a sensation of being constantly watched. This perception, though not "proof" in the traditional sense, is very significant subjective evidence. Spirituality, after all, operates not by laboratory criteria, but by laws of vibration and consciousness. When the individual persistently feels something extra, something escaping reason but clearly present in their inner life, they should trust this instinct and seek help.

It is at this point that faith and spiritual knowledge walk side by side. Recognizing an astral clone doesn't happen through external imposition, but by the soul's openness to truth. Each physical symptom, each strange thought, each repetitive dream forms a mosaic of clues. And when the picture completes, consciousness awakens. The person realizes they are not imagining, not crazy, not alone. There is, indeed, a presence. There is a reflection of them walking alongside, a being born of them, but now needing reintegration, dissolution, or liberation.

Spiritual detection, therefore, is a process of internal illumination. It's the moment truth's light penetrates the hidden layers of existence and reveals what was hidden. Detecting an astral clone is like turning on a flashlight in a dark room: the form appears, contours reveal themselves, fear dissipates. For the clone's greatest power lies in ignorance—and its greatest weakness, in consciousness. When the human being looks within and recognizes their shadow, it loses dominance. And then the true healing process begins.

Chapter 21
Initial Preparation

The presence of an astral clone represents more than a simple energetic anomaly: it reflects a complex interaction between repressed aspects of the psyche, unintegrated emotional fragments, and vibrational patterns perpetuated in the unconscious. The realization of its existence reveals a subtle but deep fissure in the individual's energetic structure, pointing to the urgent need for internal reorganization. It is not an isolated problem, but the manifestation of imbalances accumulated over time, demanding conscious and structured confrontation. The effective approach to this reality begins with personal preparation on multiple levels—spiritual, emotional, mental, and physical— recognizing that the process of liberation from an astral clone is, above all, a process of integral restoration of the being.

This preparation starts with understanding that a person's energy field acts as a mirror of their inner life. Everything cultivated in the mind and heart reverberates in this field, which, in turn, directly influences the experienced reality. When the astral clone manifests, it denounces a frequency maintained actively long enough to condense into an autonomous form, albeit dependent on the host. This form did not arise by chance: it was nurtured, consciously or unconsciously, by unresolved pains, crystallized emotional patterns, and habits distorting the natural energy flow. Therefore, before any attempt at rupture, it is imperative to strengthen the connection with the higher self, expand inner lucidity, and restore vibrational alignment with the forces of light, so that fragmentation gives way to integration.

This preparatory process demands deep commitment to one's own healing process. It is not enough to acquire theoretical knowledge or perform superficial practices. It is necessary to dive honestly into the most hidden layers of consciousness, rescue parts of the soul left behind, take responsibility for internal creations, and initiate an inner reform based on high values. Preparation requires constancy, surrender, and sensitivity to perceive subtle signs indicating progress or resistance. It is in this scenario that the indispensable vibrational foundation is built to face the clone not as an enemy to be exterminated, but as a creation to be understood, transcended, and finally, liberated.

This initial preparation is more than a protocol; it is the recognition that the spiritual field needs strengthening, protection, and cleansing before attempting to cut the tie with an entity that, even being a projection of the self, has developed survival instincts and, in many cases, resistance. The astral clone, especially those molded by traumas, emotional addictions, or dense energies, acts like a living creature: it feels, thinks, and, to some extent, fights to maintain its existence. Breaking away from it without adequate preparation can generate deeper imbalances, relapses, or intense reactions beyond the practitioner's control.

The first step in this preparation consists of establishing an inner state of constant vigilance. This implies attentive observation of one's own thoughts, emotions, and behaviors, without judgment, but with the firm intention of understanding which mental patterns feed or reinforce the clone's presence. This exercise is similar to watching a garden where weeds grow: it's not enough to pull them out—one must understand how they form, where their roots come from, and what feeds them. The inattentive mind is fertile ground for repeating old patterns. The clone, as an extension of these patterns, strengthens in the unconscious routine.

Simultaneously, raising personal vibration is essential. The astral clone only survives in lower vibrational ranges, feeding on fear, anger, resentment, guilt, or any other state weakening the auric field and reducing energetic frequency. It feeds on emotional pain dragging on unresolved, on unhealed grievances, on recurring thoughts sabotaging faith and self-esteem. It exists where there is stagnation and darkness. Therefore, vibrational elevation is a movement of liberation. Reading elevated spiritual texts, practicing inner silence, listening to harmonic music, meditating, praying, being in contact with nature, and doing good—all are ways to reconnect with the most luminous within oneself and gradually weaken the density sustaining the clone.

Caring for the body is also part of the preparation. The body is the soul's instrument of manifestation, and any spiritual practice excluding it is incomplete. A lighter, natural diet, with fresh, living foods, favors energy field cleansing. Avoiding excesses, alcoholic beverages, toxic substances, and environments charged with negativity is equally important. Some spiritual masters even recommend short, conscious fasts—not as punishment, but as an exercise in mastering impulses and physical purification. Ingesting fluidified water, consecrated with prayers and elevated intentions, is also a traditional practice to prepare the organism and the subtle field.

During this preparatory period, sleep protection must be intensified. As the clone acts more freely when the physical body rests and consciousness unfolds, the bedroom environment must be transformed into a true vibrational sanctuary. Cleansing incenses like white sage, frankincense, or myrrh can be used before sleep. Crystals like amethyst and black tourmaline can be placed under the pillow or beside the bed. Praying before sleep, asking for support and protection, is more than a religious tradition: it's a powerful energetic act activating subtle defense forces. Visualizing a sphere of golden light enveloping the entire body upon lying down is a simple and effective technique to keep unwanted presences away during sleep.

The external environment must also be prepared. It is necessary to clean the house, both physically and energetically. A dirty, messy, dark, and stuffy house tends to accumulate thought-forms, astral larvae, and other miasmas that unconsciously reinforce the clone's action. Organizing spaces, opening windows, letting sunlight in, getting rid of broken objects or those carrying painful memories are symbolic and practical actions transforming the residence's energy field. Additionally, smudging with herbs, using coarse salt water in corners, and playing mantras or sacred chants softly in denser environments can be employed.

During this period, writing is also recommended. Yes, writing. Recording thoughts, emotions, dreams, recurring patterns. This spiritual diary will serve as a mirror of the soul, revealing what conscious discourse often ignores. One can even write letters to the clone—not with rancor, but with the intention of understanding. Telling it what it represents, why it was created, what caused its formation, and how the time has come to release it. Writing to heal. Writing to reveal what was hidden. Writing is a powerful tool for self-transformation, because naming what one feels takes power away from the shadow.

Another important point in this preparation is the commitment to one's own healing. Facing an astral clone is facing oneself. Trying to dissolve the clone while continuing to repeat the same behaviors, cultivate the same resentments, feed the same fears is futile. One must deeply desire liberation. And this desire cannot be superficial. It must be born from the soul's center, from the unwavering decision to no longer live in energetic captivity. This commitment translates into daily attitudes, small choices, conscious acts that, summed up, create the necessary strength to sustain the dissolution process.

It should be understood that this preparation has no exact deadline. For some, a week suffices. For others, it may take months. Each being carries a distinct history, vibration, and energetic structure. There is no rush, as it is not a race against time, but a journey towards wholeness. And the more solid this preparatory base, the more effective the process of separating from the clone will be. It's like sharpening the sword before battle: not out of fear, but wisdom.

At the end of this phase, the energy field will be cleaner, the mind calmer, the heart lighter. The shadow previously hiding in the unconscious corners will begin becoming visible. And the strengthened being can then initiate practices aimed at the definitive dissolution of the astral clone—not with fear or hesitation, but with the certainty of being ready to reclaim their sacred inner space. Preparation is not just the beginning: it is the foundation upon which all liberation will be built.

Chapter 22
Spiritual Cleansing

Spiritual cleansing emerges as one of the deepest and most transformative movements within the being's liberation process. After consolidating a firm and elevated inner base, the individual finds themselves fit to perform energetic interventions that not only remove vibrational impurities but also dismantle the hidden foundations sustaining the astral clone's presence. This stage transcends superficial rituals or automated gestures: it invites total presence, lucid intention, and a loving commitment to one's own liberation. Each action performed in this context becomes a sacred act, representing the reappropriation of the inner space long occupied by distorted energy forms, created in moments of emotional fragility or spiritual disconnection.

This process demands conscious surrender and respect for the subtle laws governing spiritual fields. True cleansing only occurs when there is a genuine call for light, when the being, entirely, wishes to be vibrationally reborn. It is in this state of surrender that practices gain strength: herbs release their living essence, crystals amplify their frequency, sacred sounds reverberate like swords of light, and water carries away what no longer serves the soul's purpose. More than dissolving the clone's presence, this stage reveals how much the being was often accustomed to living with their own shadow without realizing it. Spiritual cleansing, in this context, acts as a mirror, revealing what needs transmutation and offering tools for it to occur with clarity and firmness.

By embracing this process, the practitioner begins noticing subtle yet profound changes in perception, feelings, and the quality of their presence. The emerging lightness is not just physical—it touches higher dimensions of consciousness, awakening a new relationship with the body, environment, and the sacred. Spiritual cleansing is, therefore, not an isolated event, but a continuous reconnection with essence. Each layer of density dissolving opens space for inner truth to flourish, pushing the clone away not with violence, but with light—a light that, once lit, makes impossible the permanence of that which lives off darkness.

Spiritual cleansing cannot be done hastily or carelessly. It requires presence, firm intention, and an open heart. Every gesture, every word, every instrument used must be imbued with consciousness. After all, we are talking about a process dealing with subtle vibrational layers, where thought-forms, crystallized emotions, fragments of pain, and astral connections operate. In this scenario, the astral clone survives as a hidden parasite, feeding on what accumulates untransformed. Therefore, the objective here is not just removing dirt, but opening the way for light to circulate and dissolve what does not belong to the being.

One of the oldest and most effective ways to initiate spiritual cleansing is smudging with herbs. Since time immemorial, plants have been recognized as living entities, endowed with specific vibrational properties. Burning white sage, rosemary, rue, or lavender, for example, is not just an aromatherapy practice—it's an act of invoking the natural powers of purification. The smoke from these herbs, when directed with clear intention, penetrates the invisible pores of the aura, breaking dense links, disaggregating astral larvae, and creating a temporary protective field. When smudging one's own body, perform upward movements, from floor to head, visualizing all dark energy being released and transmuted. In environments, cover all corners, including under beds, behind doors, inside closets. Dark and stuffy places tend to accumulate entities and stagnant forms supporting the clone vibrationally.

Another fundamental practice is energetic cleansing baths. One of the classics involves preparing an infusion with coarse salt, rue leaves, rosemary, and basil. After the usual hygienic bath, this mixture should be poured from the neck down, never over the head, while silently praying for all negativity to be washed away. The effect is immediate: many report feeling lightness, relief, or even a slight shiver—a sign that dense charges have shifted. It's important not to towel dry after this bath, but allow the skin to air dry, absorbing the properties of the water and herbs.

Besides baths and smudging, conscious use of crystals can potentiate spiritual cleansing. Crystals like black tourmaline, obsidian, amethyst, and clear quartz possess properties of absorption, transmutation, and energetic amplification. Placing them on the chakras during meditation creates a resonance vortex assisting in dissolving energetic blocks. Tourmaline, for example, is excellent for the root chakra, acting as an anchor expelling harmful vibrations. Amethyst, linked to the crown chakra, favors connection with higher planes and acts as a mental purifier. These crystals should be energized before use, preferably with water and sun, and programmed with the specific intention of cleansing and protection.

The power of the word also cannot be underestimated. Prayers, mantras, invocations, and affirmations act as sound frequencies reordering the being's vibrational matrix. Reciting mantras like "Om Mani Padme Hum," "Om Namah Shivaya," or even traditional Christian prayers like Psalm 91 or the Prayer to Saint Michael the Archangel, creates a sound wave reverberating through all dimensions of the spiritual field. These words, when spoken with faith, cut dense links, disintegrate thought-forms, and weaken the astral clone's energetic structure. Daily repetition of a prayer or mantra is like a shield forming, layer by layer, around the practitioner.

It's also important to care for the environment's vibrational cleanliness. Houses and rooms where sadness, fights, dense thoughts, or disorganization accumulate tend to generate an atmosphere conducive to entities and thought-forms. Home cleansing should include organizing spaces, removing unused objects, opening windows for sunlight, and using instruments like bells, Tibetan bowls, or even rhythmic clapping to move stagnant energy. Sound is a powerful astral cleaner, capable of breaking energetic shells often supporting the clone in environments.

A lesser-known but extremely effective practice is using protective circles with coarse salt. One can draw a circle of salt on the floor around oneself while affirming: "Nothing that is not of the light can cross this limit." This symbolic gesture has profound energetic value, representing the establishment of vibrational boundaries. The astral clone, confronted with barriers of light and order, begins destabilizing. It feeds on disorder, chaos, unconscious repetition. Any conscious act of spiritual organization is a direct attack on its sustenance.

During the cleansing period, reactions are common. There might be intense dreams, exhaustion, sudden melancholy episodes, or even physical manifestations like headaches, nausea, or chills. These symptoms should not be feared: they are signs density is moving, the process is working. It's spiritual mud being removed. It's crucial, in these moments, to maintain serenity and continue practices, knowing each discomfort is temporary and part of purification.

Always end cleansing sessions with positive visualizations. Imagining oneself enveloped in white or golden light, feeling this light penetrate every cell, every empty space of the body, filling and healing, is essential to seal the energy field. This visualization reinforces the practice's purpose, removes any lingering residue attempting to remain, and prepares the ground for the next steps, involving banishment, bond cutting, and reintegration of self-sovereignty.

Cleansing oneself spiritually is an act of courage and self-love. It's affirming to the universe: "I no longer accept carrying what is not mine, I no longer accept living with what hurts me." It's a rite of passage marking the beginning of definitive separation between the essential being and the shadow imitating it. And when this decision is made firmly, the astral clone, having inhabited the soul's basements for so long, begins realizing its time is ending.

Chapter 23
Banishing Ritual

The banishing ritual represents the culmination of a process of reclaiming inner power and reaffirming spiritual sovereignty. After removing the dense layers feeding the astral clone's presence, the moment arrives to declare, with authority and clarity, that no dissociated energy or autonomous form has permission anymore to remain in the being's vibrational field. Banishing is, therefore, a ceremony of empowerment, where the individual positions themselves as a conscious guardian of their own energetic space, breaking the final bonds with what imprisoned them and restoring their inner centrality. This practice is not an empty mystical artifice, but a concrete act of reintegration, in which the spirit rises and assumes its original place in the subtle order of existence.

This ritualistic action goes beyond expelling presences or interferences: it alters the vibrational codes sustaining unconscious connections, undoing silent energetic pacts, compulsive mental habits, and emotional frequencies that, even without deliberate intention, kept alive the tie with the astral clone. By banishing these forms, the practitioner is not just sending away an external fragment—they are cutting the internal root sustaining this manifestation. This requires more than symbolic gestures: it demands alignment between thought, emotion, and spirit. Every word pronounced, every visualization, every movement during the ritual must express the conviction that that cycle has ended. Presence is key: when the being is whole in the gesture, energy obeys, and the field reorganizes according to the newly decreed order.

The banishing's strength is directly linked to the practitioner's authenticity. It's unnecessary to adopt complex forms or repeat hermetic formulas if these don't resonate with one's inner truth. What makes banishing effective is clear intention and vibrational certainty that liberation is possible—and happening. The being standing before themselves and affirming, with a firm voice, that their space is sacred and inviolable, activates higher forces responding immediately to this call. The astral clone, whose existence depends on energetic breaches and resonances with states of fragility, finds no more sustenance when confronted with this conscious light. Thus, the banishing ritual becomes not just a final act of expulsion, but the beginning of a new stage: living fully anchored in oneself, free from the distortion that once made itself present, but finds no home anymore.

A true banishing ritual acts as a vibrational decree. When performed with full consciousness, it not only wards off unwanted entities or energetic forms but also dissolves the frequencies allowing their permanence. In the case of the astral clone, banishing is the direct rupture of its connection. It cuts the channels through which energy flowed between the original being and its duplicate, interrupts the accesses the clone used to influence, drain, or manipulate. More than expulsion, banishing is a vibrational repositioning: the sacred self places itself at the center and reclaims its inner space with authority.

There isn't a single correct way to banish. What matters is the combination of three elements: firm intention, conscious presence, and symbolic ritualistic action. Some traditions use precise formulas, like the Lesser Banishing Ritual of the Pentagram from the Golden Dawn, tracing symbols in the air in four directions, invoking divine names vibrating on higher planes. Others prefer simpler yet equally powerful rituals, like using sound (bell, drum, mantra), fire (candle, incense), words (affirmations, verbal commands), and gestures (hand movements, use of a wand or athame).

An example of an accessible and effective banishing can be performed as follows: the practitioner stands in the center of a clean room, preferably after smudging. Barefoot touching the ground, breathes deeply, visualizes a sphere of white light enveloping their entire body. Then, extends the dominant hand (or holds a ritual wand, if available) and traces in the air, before them, a symbol of power—could be a pentagram, cross, star, or any other sacred icon of their faith. While doing this, pronounces in a firm, clear voice: "In the name of the supreme light dwelling within me, I banish every presence, form, or energy not of my divine essence! May every tie with what limits, drains, or imprisons me, be now cut, undone, and transmuted!"

The practitioner then turns clockwise, repeating the gesture and words for the other cardinal directions: east, south, west, north. At each point, reinforces their intention firmly, like stating an absolute truth. To intensify the process, one can create a circle of coarse salt around themselves before starting, representing the barrier between self and the external world. Using a white candle lit at the circle's center also helps anchor the luminous presence.

The power of sound is an indispensable ally in banishing. Rhythmic clapping, playing a bell, a shamanic drum, or even pronouncing sacred sounds like the mantra "Om," "Ra," "Aum," or archaic words like "Agla," "Tetragrammaton," or "Adonai," according to the adopted esoteric tradition, create a resonance fragmenting and expelling dissonant entities or vibrational forms. Sound is pure vibration—and as such, molds, expands, and purifies subtle fields.

Water can also be employed as a banishing element. A simple preparation involves mixing water with coarse salt and a few drops of lavender or rosemary essential oil. This solution, fluidified with a prayer or consecration, can be sprinkled in house corners and around the body with a small herb broom, fingers, or even a plant sprig. Each drop carries the force of cleansing intention. At the end, a prayer sealing the act reinforces the command: "May light remain where shadow once was. May only the good, beautiful, and true inhabit this sacred space."

In more advanced banishments, like those used in ceremonial rituals, there's direct invocation of higher entities. The practitioner, duly protected and aligned, can call upon the presence of guides, archangels, ascended masters, or their Higher Self, asking for help in cutting ties and dissipating autonomous forms. In these cases, visions, shivers, chills, or even momentary physical manifestations like dizziness or yawning are common. This shouldn't frighten: it's a sign the field is being purged, the banished entity is detaching from the energy system.

It's important to understand banishing isn't a definitive solution by itself. It acts as an emergency intervention or pattern break, but if the inner pattern originating the astral clone isn't transformed, the form might try returning or be recreated. Therefore, after banishing, maintaining high vibration, continuing protection practices, and strengthening the newly achieved state of consciousness is indispensable. The astral clone is a product of resonance: if the previous frequency persists, it might find ways to reconnect.

Many report that after a well-executed banishing, there's an immediate sense of relief—as if an invisible pressure dissipated, air felt lighter, body looser, mind clearer. Others experience revealing dreams, symbolic visions, or strong intuitions that something important was broken. These signs indicate the ritual succeeded, but also point the work must continue. Each cut thread needs replacement with roots of light, new connections with what elevates and strengthens.

Some practitioners prefer performing banishing in cycles—for example, for seven consecutive days or for three days at specific times, like dawn or dusk. This type of repetition creates a kind of energetic seal, hindering the return of unwanted influences. Discipline is an essential part of the process. The astral clone is persistent, especially if it existed for a long time. But the strength of awakened will is infinitely greater.

The most important thing in any banishing ritual is faith. Not blind faith, but the conviction you have authority over your vibrational field, that no external force can command your thoughts, emotions, or energies anymore. The astral clone, facing a conscious and determined being, begins destabilizing. It depends on doubt, fragility, and distraction to survive. But confronted by a firm spirit, enveloped in light, it finds no more shelter. The banishing ritual is, then, the proclamation of freedom. It's the moment the being looks within, sees their own strength, and says: "Here, in this temple that is me, there is no more place for what disintegrates me. Only light dwells in me now." And this truth, affirmed courageously, echoes through all planes of being, sealing the door through which the astral clone once entered.

Chapter 24
Spiritual Protection

Spiritual protection establishes itself as the invisible yet fundamental foundation sustaining the achieved liberation and preventing any attempt at vibrational regression. After banishment, where ties with the astral clone are consciously broken, a new phase begins where maintaining the elevated energy field becomes an absolute priority. This protection is not a static shield but a dynamic, living field, continually renewed through spiritual discipline, mental vigilance, and daily cultivation of inner light. The true power of protection arises from alignment between thought, emotion, and action, creating an internal environment inhospitable to any dissonant frequency. Thus, it's not just about warding off external influences, but establishing a vibrational pattern so coherent and elevated that no force incompatible with light can attach itself there.

This stage requires spiritual maturity and an active stance towards one's own existence. True protection stems from ethical commitment to one's evolution, conscious choice of edifying thoughts, healing emotions, and illuminating actions. When the being understands every energetic breach reflects an internal imbalance—be it an unresolved judgment, persistent resentment, or silently nurtured doubt—they begin treating protection not as defense against the external, but as continuous work of purification and internal coherence. It's at this point the aura strengthens, becoming a true spiritual force field. And this fortress isn't built by chance: it's constructed daily with conscious choices, aligned words, inner silence, and connection with the highest.

In this expanded state of consciousness, the being awakens to the fact that spiritual self-protection is, actually, an act of self-love in its highest form. It's the decision to no longer allow one's light to be extinguished by low-vibration forces, nor by self-sabotaging attitudes reactivating old patterns. Protection thus becomes an expression of achieved sovereignty, a reflection of clarity from someone no longer accepting to yield space to what imbalances, hurts, or weakens. And the more this stance takes root in daily life—in simple gestures, heartfelt prayers, clean and harmonized environments—the more impassable the energy field becomes, naturally repelling any attempt by the astral clone to reintegrate or by thought-forms that once found dwelling in the void of unconsciousness.

Protecting oneself spiritually isn't living in paranoia or a permanent state of defensive alert. On the contrary, it's inhabiting a vibrational field so elevated, coherent, and cohesive that no dissonant energy can remain there long. The secret to true protection lies in balance: not closing oneself off from the world, but being so centered and internally illuminated that external forces lose their power of influence. The astral clone, as we've seen, cannot sustain itself in the presence of full light—it requires shadow, distraction, emotional imbalance. Thus, by cultivating light within, the human being becomes inviolable.

The first element of this protection is the mental shield. Recurring thoughts of guilt, fear, inferiority, or anger open invisible fissures in the psychosphere, through which opportunistic influences and entities penetrate. Therefore, vigilance over thoughts is one of the deepest foundations of spiritual protection. This doesn't mean repressing or denying feelings, but transforming them lucidly. When a negative thought arises, welcome it, understand its origin, and consciously redirect the energy. Repeating positive affirmations, like "I am light in constant expansion" or "No external force has power over me," helps reprogram the mind and consolidate the new vibrational pattern.

Creative visualization is another powerful instrument. Every day upon waking, dedicate a few minutes to imagining a sphere of light enveloping the body. This sphere can be golden, white, blue, or whatever color intuition indicates. Visualize it pulsating with high frequency, automatically warding off anything dissonant. Feel this light penetrating your chakras, strengthening energy centers, creating an indestructible vibrational armor. Before sleep, repeat the process. This protects the body during sleep, when we are more susceptible to astral interferences.

Consecrated objects also act as protection anchors. Amulets, stones, religious or spiritual symbols have the power to condense a specific frequency and radiate it continuously. A black tourmaline, for example, when cleansed and programmed, can absorb and transmute negative energies. An amethyst aids spiritual connection and mind purification. A Saint Benedict medal, crucifix, Star of David, or pentagram, when used with faith and respect, become true protection portals. The important thing is these objects are chosen with the heart and consecrated with a personal ritual—even simple—invoking light and determining their protective function.

Furthermore, prayer—regardless of religion—is an irreplaceable tool. A praying soul is connected to higher sources, aligned with good, and this in itself wards off dense entities. Prayers like the Our Father, Hail Mary, Psalm 23, or specific formulas like the "Prayer to Saint Michael the Archangel," should be chanted with feeling and conviction. The "21-day Prayer to Archangel Michael," for example, is widely known for its effectiveness in dissolving negative spiritual ties, including bonds with astral clones. Over three weeks, the practitioner daily affirms their will for liberation, invoking Michael's sword of light to cut everything not belonging to their divine field.

Music also plays an essential role. Harmonic sounds, mantras, devotional chants, and healing binaural frequencies contribute to keeping the environment and aura in an elevated state. A simple sequence of notes can destabilize an intrusive entity's frequency, making it unable to sustain itself in that field. Mantras like "Om Mani Padme Hum," "Gayatri," "Om Namah Shivaya," or Gregorian chants, played daily at home, transform the environment into a dwelling of light.

The physical space we live in must be continuously purified. Incense, periodic smudging with sage, myrrh, or rosemary, herb baths, using coarse salt in corners, and lit candles with protection prayers are simple practices keeping the house's vibration elevated. Harmony at home—silence, respect, beauty, music, order—is also part of spiritual protection. Chaotic or emotionally charged environments are the preferred habitat of unwanted astral forms.

Another protection resource is connection with spiritual guides. Many people are unaware of or neglect the presence of these loving, wise beings accompanying each soul on its evolutionary journey. By talking to them—in prayers, letters, meditations—this bond strengthens, opening a channel for communication and aid. Guides don't interfere uninvited. But when called, they manifest in various ways: sudden intuitions, synchronistic encounters, revealing dreams. They act as living shields, sustaining light when our strength seems depleted.

There's also a little-discussed but extremely effective resource: spiritual fasting. Reserving one day a week to not consume animal products, avoid excessive distractions, cultivate silence and introspection is a way to subtilize the energy field and allow the spirit to take command. On this day, dedicate time to spiritual reading, meditation, intuitive writing. The subtle field appreciates and strengthens.

Importantly, no spiritual protection works if there's contradiction between external practice and internal attitude. That is, doing baths, prayers, and smudging is futile if the heart continues nurturing hatred, envy, resentment, or judgment. These emotions open doors no herb or prayer can seal. Protecting oneself spiritually is above all an ethical commitment to oneself. It's a pact of lucidity. It's choosing, day after day, to feed only what is good, beautiful, and true.

With active and well-cared-for spiritual protection, the astral clone—if still trying to approach—will find an inaccessible vibrational field. It will begin dissolving due to lack of energetic sustenance. Moreover: other entities previously surrounding the person's auric field, exploiting breaches, will also move away. The aura becomes like a wall of light, within which peace, discernment, and true freedom flourish.

This stage, though seemingly passive, is one of the most powerful of the entire journey. It's the invisible shield guaranteeing the permanence of achieved liberation. And it's also the sign the being has definitively assumed sovereignty of their light. Because one who protects themselves with love and consciousness no longer fears—they simply live, vibrate, and shine.

Chapter 25
Spiritual Help

The journey of spiritual liberation, however intense and disciplined, at certain moments encounters barriers requiring the summoning of forces beyond individual capacity. Spiritual help emerges as a legitimate and necessary resource when, even after consistent practices of purification, protection, and banishment, the astral clone's presence persists with force, resistance, or dissimulation. This assistance should not be seen as a sign of personal insufficiency, but as the highest expression of wisdom: recognizing there are times when intervention by more experienced consciousnesses, or trained spiritual collectives, is essential to dissolve ingrained patterns or complex interferences challenging the reach of individual will. Opening oneself to this assistance is an act of trust in divine support and a crucial step to deepen the healing process.

The search for spiritual help, when done with discernment and surrender, expands possibilities for reconnecting with the sacred. The being, by exiting vibrational isolation and connecting to broader currents of healing, enters an invisible support network operating subtly and effectively. Each spiritual line, each religious or esoteric tradition, offers its own instruments to intervene in the energy field, often accessing dimensions and interference levels the practitioner alone could not overcome. This movement of approaching other knowledge is not just functional—it's also symbolic, marking the decision to transcend the ego, abandon the silent pride preventing many from receiving help, and allow light to arrive through diverse means, including through the outstretched hand of other incarnate beings.

In this context, accepting help from guides, therapists, mediums, masters, or spiritual groups is more than resorting to an external solution—it's integrating a new frequency of belonging. It's knowing oneself part of a compassionate and intelligent whole, where healing circulates among those willing to share their gifts. This surrender opens doors, dissolves internal resistances, and accelerates the astral clone's disintegration, which loses not only energetic sustenance but also the psychic resonance keeping it tied to the practitioner's field. And thus, enveloped by currents of loving aid and sustained by high-vibration spiritual presences, the being rediscovers the strength to continue their journey with more lightness, clarity, and depth, towards the fullness of their original essence.

Spiritual assistance can come from various sources, all valid as long as connected to light and conducted seriously. Spiritist centers, Umbanda and Candomblé terreiros, apometry houses, Christian churches, Buddhist communities, meditation groups, Reiki masters, holistic therapists, shamans, healers—the world is full of human and spiritual channels dedicated to assisting suffering souls. It's not about religion, but attunement: the person should seek the spiritual line resonating with their soul and inspiring trust. When this connection happens, the liberation process tends to accelerate and deepen.

In Kardecist Spiritist centers, for example, there are specific disobsession sessions to deal with entities linked to the incarnates' perispirit. Although the term "astral clone" isn't present in Kardecist codification, many mediums and indoctrinators have dealt with cases where an energetic fragment or thought-form strongly linked to the patient needed forwarding or dissolution. In these sessions, the spiritual team—composed of mentors and rescuers—acts directly on the double's structure, identifying its links, cutting fluidic cords, and forwarding the form to recovery centers on the astral plane. The incarnate's work is to remain in prayer, faith, and vigilance, as even after detachment, there's a rebalancing phase requiring vibrational support.

In Umbanda terreiros, treatment is usually more vigorous and direct. Spiritual guides like caboclos, pretos-velhos, and light exus use intense energetic passes, smudging, and incorporations to identify and remove not only clones but also larvae, magic, pacts, and fragmentations. In these environments, guides not only remove the intruder but also give specific guidance to the querent: herb baths, prayers, offerings, behavioral changes. It's a purification process affecting body, mind, and spirit. Many cases of strongly rooted astral clones are successfully treated in these spaces, as guides have authority and deep knowledge about the world of autonomous forms and energies.

Apometry, in turn, is a highly specialized and systematized technique for dealing with complex cases like astral cloning. In apometric sessions, mediums unfold under the coordinator's command and, together with mentors, locate the clone in parallel dimensions. Often, these forms are hidden in vibrational pockets, encapsulated by obsessors, or even connected to astral equipment like chips and remote control devices. The spiritual team then performs detailed operations: detaching the clone, dissolving it by transmutation, sending the form to regeneration chambers or vibrational disposal, depending on its nature. It's also common to find, alongside the clone, other parasitic forms—like subpersonalities, miasmas, past life pacts—removed in the same process. Apometry is a surgical tool, and when applied by well-trained teams, usually results in perceptible changes in the person's field.

In Christian contexts—Catholic or Evangelical—although the concept of astral clone doesn't formally exist, many manifestations identifiable as such are treated as possessions, demonic influences, or spiritual attacks. In Catholic churches, one can resort to minor exorcisms (liberation prayer, blessings, use of sacramentals) or, in more serious cases, a formal exorcism conducted by an authorized priest. Fervent prayer, confession, communion, and personal consecration are acts that, according to this view, expel evil and restore the covenant with God. Evangelical churches follow a similar line: liberation services, laying on of hands, fasting, praise, and Bible reading are used to break links with evil forces. In both cases, intense faith and surrender to the divine function as catalysts for transformation and protection.

There are also shamanic and holistic approaches, where the therapist—often a medium and healer—acts with ancestral practices like the drum, chant, ritual dance, use of power herbs, crystals, breaths, and extractions. In these rituals, the clone is identified through visions or sensory perceptions, and the healer performs an energetic removal, often with help from their spiritual allies: power animals, ancestors, or shamanic guides. After removal, there are rites of reintegration and aura strengthening, with specific recommendations for the post-treatment period. These approaches are especially effective when the clone arose from trauma fragmentation or was created in past life contexts, as they access cellular memories and deep fields of being.

Still within the holistic field, there are therapists specialized in vibrational treatments like Reiki, Pranic Healing, ThetaHealing, spiritual family constellation, and other approaches. Although subtler, these techniques work directly with the person's bioenergetic field, dissolving blockages and restoring vibrational fluidity. In Reiki sessions, for example, it's common for the therapist to feel or visualize strange forms linked to the patient—often corresponding to clones, subpersonalities, or dense thought-forms. The laying on of hands channels healing energy weakening and dissolving these aggregates, while simultaneously strengthening the healthy energetic structure.

Another important aspect of spiritual help is psychological therapeutic support. Many astral clones feed on traumas, repetitive mental patterns, states of victimization, or self-sabotage. An experienced therapist can help the individual identify these patterns, reframe them, and transform them. Past life therapy, for example, allows the patient to access the origin of certain energetic bonds and heal them at the root. Family constellation, in turn, shows how inherited patterns can influence the energy field and give rise to fragmentations resulting in clones. Transpersonal psychologists, integrating spirituality into the clinical process, are especially recommended in these cases.

Seeking spiritual help, therefore, is opening oneself to healing on all levels: physical, emotional, mental, and spiritual. It's allowing other hands—visible and invisible—to assist in reconstructing the true self. Pride, fear, or disbelief are the main obstacles in this process. Many resist for fear of judgment, not understanding what's happening to them, or not wanting to acknowledge they are being influenced. But by taking the first step and asking for help, a new flow establishes: the universe responds, guides approach, the path begins clearing. There is no complete cure without support. And when this support is chosen with discernment and accepted with gratitude, the process of dissolving the astral clone not only accelerates but becomes deeper and more transformative. The person then feels they are no longer alone. They walk surrounded by allies, by invisible lights sustaining them and celebrating each step towards total liberation.

Chapter 26
Shamanic Healing

Shamanic healing represents one of the deepest and oldest paths for soul reintegration and dissolution of dissociated forces, such as the astral clone. Rooted in traditions recognizing the human being as an indivisible part of the cosmic whole and in constant relation with the spiritual, natural, and ancestral worlds, this practice relies on symbolic listening to the wounded soul, seeking to understand, welcome, and reintegrate the parts that detached from it throughout the journey. Unlike approaches focused solely on expelling or combating intrusive energetic forms, shamanism understands that every imbalance carries an origin, a memory, a reason. The astral clone, seen from this perspective, is not just an invader: it is an autonomous expression of a pain still unresolved—and therefore needs listening before release.

On this healing path, the shaman acts as an intermediary between worlds, navigating the invisible dimensions where lost soul fragments reside. Their sensitivity, strengthened by rituals, inner silence, and connection with their spiritual allies, allows them to identify the origin and nature of the imbalance manifesting as a clone. As they access spiritual planes, they not only perceive what is displaced but also dialogue with the parts of the soul marginalized, frightened, or forgotten. This spiritual listening is a sacred art: it requires empathy, intuition, and profound respect for the stories each fragment carries. Healing, then, doesn't happen as forced elimination, but as loving reconciliation between the being seeking healing and the parts of themselves left behind, crystallized in dissociated energetic forms.

The impact of this reintegration is immediate and often moving. The return of the soul fragment—whether through retrieval or extraction of an implanted entity—represents a new beginning. The person's vibrational field reorganizes, energy centers regain balance, and new emotional and spiritual clarity emerges. It's not just about feeling better: it's about feeling whole. The astral clone's dissolution, in this process, is not an abrupt end, but the natural conclusion of a story that found listening, acceptance, and transcendence. And the person undergoing this experience doesn't return to being the same: they return more connected to their essence, firmer on their path, and more conscious that true healing arises from the loving reunion with all their parts.

For shamans, the human being is not an indivisible entity. They are composed of soul parts that can, under certain circumstances, separate from the whole. This separation occurs especially in the face of intense traumas, deep fears, emotional shocks, or negative rituals. When a piece of the soul departs, it can get stuck on some plane of the spiritual world, sometimes remaining there for years, decades, or entire lifetimes. This fragment, by remaining active and separate, tends to acquire an autonomous energetic life, with its own identity, although based on the original soul matrix. This is what we now call an astral clone, but which in shamanic understanding is a broken-spirit needing to be brought back.

The best-known and most revered technique for dealing with this issue is soul retrieval. In this ritual, the shaman, after ritualistic preparation and trance induction—usually by the repetitive sound of the drum or rattle—embarks on a spiritual journey to the invisible worlds. These worlds are described as layers of reality: the lower world (associated with ancestry and traumas), the middle world (related to daily life), and the upper world (domain of spirit guides and healing). Upon identifying where the lost fragment is located, the shaman dialogues with it, observes its form—which could be a wounded child, a caged animal, a shadow—and, with help from their spiritual allies, convinces this soul part to return to the querent's body. The return is sealed with a ritualistic breath: the shaman blows the fragment back, usually into the crown (crown chakra) or center of the chest (heart chakra) of the person, while chanting sacred songs and asking the Great Spirit's permission for reintegration. This symbolic gesture not only reintegrates the fragment but dissolves the astral clone created from it, as the energetic matrix sustaining its existence has been reabsorbed. After the ritual, the person usually reports feelings of completeness, clarity, lightness, and, in some cases, intense crying, as if rediscovering an essential part of themselves forgotten.

There is also shamanic extraction, used when the intrusive form—in this case, the astral clone—is not a legitimate soul fragment, but an externally created entity implanted in the person's field. This occurs, for example, in cases of negative magic, involuntary pacts, or astral manipulations. In these scenarios, the clone is perceived as an invader, a dense mass, or a dark presence embedded somewhere in the auric field. The shaman, then, in trance, locates the insertion point, identifies the entity's nature, and, with ritualistic movements, extracts it. This extraction can occur in various ways: pulling with hands, using instruments like crystals, feathers, wands, or even through suction—an ancient and potent practice where the shaman symbolically sucks the entity out through the mouth and then spits it into a container with water, alcohol, or herbs, which is then burned or ceremonially discarded. After removal, the person's field is sealed with herb smoke, chants, and invocation of spiritual guardians. In some cases, the shaman also rebalances the chakras and offers a protective spirit—power animal, ancestor, or elemental guardian—to watch over the space left by the intruder.

The effectiveness of these practices depends not only on the healer's skill but also on the patient's surrender. Shamanism requires the individual to participate in the process with sincerity and reverence. Often, the shaman recommends a period of retreat after the ritual, with dietary restrictions, alcohol abstinence, meditation, and specific herb baths. They might also suggest creating a home altar, where the person deposits daily intentions of light, as a way to energetically seal the reintegration.

It's important to understand that, for shamanism, everything manifesting spiritually has a reason. An astral clone, even if disturbing, carries a message: something was forgotten, hurt, or repressed. Therefore, the shamanic process seeks not just to eliminate the form—it seeks to understand its origin, heal the pain generating it, and restore soul integrity. The clone, in this context, is not an enemy to be destroyed, but a messenger of imbalance. And when its message is heard with the heart, it dissolves like mist in the sun.

Accounts from those who underwent true shamanic healing are often marked by poetry and intensity. Many speak of revealing dreams in subsequent nights, feelings of rebirth, rediscovering forgotten memories, and a new sense of purpose. Others claim to have felt the touch of invisible hands, heard chants in darkness, or seen enveloping lights. All, however, converge on one perception: something changed profoundly. And this change comes not from the shaman, but from the spirit that finally returned home.

Shamanic healing, therefore, is not just a technique—it's a reunion with the ancestral soul, with Earth's knowledge, with the wisdom of origins. When applied ethically, with preparation, and true love for the spiritual path, it has the power to liberate not only from the astral clone but from all forms of fragmentation distancing us from who we truly are. And it teaches us, above all, that no matter how lost we've become: there will always be a song, a drum, a breath guiding us back to the spirit's home.

Chapter 27
Magical Ritual

Dissolving astral entities linked to a person's energy field requires direct and conscious confrontation, supported by actions mobilizing both psyche and subtle planes. When an astral clone is deeply rooted—whether due to its creation in ancient ritualistic contexts or continuous reinforcement of mental and emotional patterns—its deactivation demands a gesture transcending logic and acting symbolically on the being's structure. Such a process cannot be reduced to generic techniques or simplified approaches; it requires deep intervention, speaking the invisible's language, a ritual action both internal and external. Magical practice, in this context, represents the bridge between the material world and subtle spheres, allowing conscious and unconscious forces to align in a real transmutation movement.

This type of ritual is not mere performative mysticism, but a psycho-energetic operation demanding presence, clarity, and firm intention of liberation. Constructing a ritual aimed at dissolving an astral double isn't based on dogmas or ready-made formulas, but on understanding the forces involved in creating and maintaining this bond. The astral clone, by nature, is a condensed reflection of dissociated aspects of the self, kept active by emotional resonances, crystallized beliefs, or unconscious energetic bonds. Facing it, therefore, is facing a part of oneself—not to deny or destroy it, but to reintegrate or dissolve it, according to its origin and function.

Magical ritual offers means for this by allowing symbols, gestures, and nature elements to be mobilized consciously, creating a force field where the practitioner's intention can operate more effectively. Choosing materials, arranging space, verbal invocation, and final gesture aren't just ceremonial details, but channels organizing energy and translating inner desire into effective action. By taking command of their own energy field and establishing, through rite, a new vibrational order, the practitioner reclaims spiritual sovereignty. Breaking away from an astral clone is, in this sense, more than warding off an unwanted presence—it's recovering dispersed parts, revoking unconscious pacts, and updating one's identity on deep levels. The ritual, symbolizing this transformation, acts as a catalyst reorganizing the field to sustain a new internal reality.

The gesture's power lies in the congruence between thought, emotion, and action. When this triad aligns, magical practice ceases being an external resource and becomes a natural extension of awakened will, capable of dissolving dense structures and restoring original vital flow. Thus, the process of undoing the clone not only ends a cycle of dissociation but inaugurates a new stage of integration and presence.

Unlike generic rites acting broadly on purification and banishment, the magical ritual directed at the astral clone specifically aims to cut the bond between original and duplicate, deprogram energetic patterns sustaining the double, and, if possible, reintegrate legitimate fragments into the person's field, dissolving what is artificial or deleterious. The ritual's effectiveness lies not in its complexity or number of elements used, but in the clarity of intention, operator's concentration, and degree of spiritual authority conducting the practice.

One of the most accessible and effective forms of this ritual is sympathetic magic, working with physical representations of involved elements. To perform it, a reserved, clean, energetically neutral space is needed—could be a room purified with incense or smudging herbs, preferably silent and dimly lit, where the operator can concentrate deeply. At the space's center, a table or altar will be the symbolic stage. The first step is crafting two representative figures: one for oneself, another for the clone. These figures can be made of wax, clay, paper, or cloth; what matters is consecration with focus and symbolism. The figure representing the practitioner should be labeled with their full name, ideally containing a strand of hair, some saliva, or a personal object energetically linking them to the image. The second figure, representing the astral clone, should be labeled "double," "shadow," "projection," or another name representing its nature. Both figures are linked by a cord or thread—symbolizing the astral tie connecting the two forms.

At the altar's center, between the figures, place a purple candle (symbol of transmutation) and, around it, crystals like amethyst, clear quartz, or black obsidian, helping absorb and transmute released energies. Using incense of myrrh, frankincense, or rue is also recommended, properties being deep cleansing and consecration.

The practitioner begins the ritual entering a meditative state. Breathes deeply, calms the mind, visualizes themselves free of any energetic duplicate. Visualizes their auric field whole, light expanded, energy centered in the present. Then, focuses on the clone figure and feels, without fear, the connection still existing between them. Acknowledges the bond, accepts the duplicate's existence, but internally affirms this tie is no longer necessary, useful, true.

With a ritual scissor (or a previously consecrated blade), the practitioner then cuts the cord joining the two figures, stating firmly: "By the power of my sovereign spirit, I now break the tie with everything false, illusory, or imposed. I free myself and free this reflection of me. May it return to nothingness or reintegrate into light, according to higher truth." Speech must come from the heart, with authority and intention. It's not the word having power, but the force behind it.

After cutting, the clone figure must be undone. If wax, let it melt slowly in the candle flame; if paper, burn it entirely; if clay, break with a hammer and bury in earth. What matters is this gesture definitively represents the form's dissolution. Simultaneously, the practitioner's figure is consecrated with a blessing gesture—can anoint the image's forehead with essential oil, place on a crystal, wrap in white cloth—and affirm: "Now I am whole. I am within myself. No part of me is lost, divided, or absent. I am one in light and truth."

Another possible, more advanced ritual is the mirror ritual. The practitioner stands before a large mirror, a lit candle between them and the reflection. The flame creates a symbolic portal between worlds. Operator stares fixedly into their own eyes and, in a light trance induced by rhythmic breathing and concentration, invokes the astral clone to manifest in the reflection. In many cases, one might feel a presence, a change in the reflected countenance, a shadow moving independently. No need for fear: the mirror is sealed by the candle, presence confined to reflection. At this moment, operator speaks to the clone with compassion and authority: "You were created by pain, fear, fragmentation. But I am no longer that. I am now. I am whole. You no longer need to exist." And, looking into the reflection's eyes, visualizes fusion between them: clone entering through eyes, descending to heart, dissolving in inner light. This ritual requires emotional preparation and visualization practice, but holds great transformative power. The candle, at the end, should burn out completely, and the mirror covered with cloth for a few hours, to avoid reverberations.

After any magical ritual, grounding is fundamental. The practitioner should eat, touch earth, bathe, move the body. This helps stabilize energy and close the field. Also recommended is noting ritual impressions, dreams possibly arising in following days, physical and psychic sensations. Often, astral clone liberation triggers deep realignment processes, where parts of the being need reorganization on a new axis.

Magical ritual, therefore, is not just symbolic act. It's direct action on the invisible plane, where spirit language understands gestures, images, intentions, archetypes. When done with integrity, it not only dissolves the clone but strengthens the true self's presence—the one not fragmenting, not getting lost, remaining whole even after the soul's darkest night.

Chapter 28
Apometric Technique

Among the most effective approaches for dealing with deep astral interferences, the apometric technique stands out for its precision, depth, and coherence with the subtle dynamics of the integral human being. Based on solid foundations uniting spiritual science, mediumistic observation, and a systematized methodology, this practice proposes a direct and conscious confrontation of structures like astral clones, whose action can extend for years, obscuring the individual's true identity and compromising their energetic and emotional balance. Apometry, in this context, offers more than a set of techniques—it represents an advanced spiritual technology recognizing the multidimensional being's complexity and acting respectfully on each layer, promoting cleansing, reintegration, and alignment. Its strength lies not only in dissolving parasitic forms but in restoring the spirit's sovereignty over its own internal domains.

Apometry's functional basis lies in understanding the human being is composed of multiple bodies, accessible, treatable, and harmonizable separately. Controlled dissociation of these bodies allows interferences, like astral clones, to be located at levels ordinary consciousness doesn't reach. With help from a trained team assisted by spiritual mentors, the process occurs structuredly, meticulously, profoundly transformatively. Commands used—verbal, mental, vibrational—function as keys accessing dimensions where the problem is anchored. More than exorcism or banishment practice, it's a lucid dive into internal mechanisms of pain and fragmentation, where each part finds listening, understanding, appropriate destiny.

The clarity with which Apometry operates allows clone treatment beyond symptom, reaching roots of energetic and psychic disturbance permitting its formation. This approach is especially relevant when the clone isn't just artificial creation but carries real aspects of the individual—repressed emotions, unresolved traumas, limiting beliefs crystallized over time. In these cases, Apometry acts sensitively, avoiding abrupt ruptures, opting for conscious reintegration. This transforms treatment into deep self-knowledge process, where the assisted not only sees themselves free from parasitic entity but rediscovers forgotten parts of themselves, promoting healing simultaneously spiritual, emotional, psychological. The technique, therefore, focuses not on destroying anomaly, but restoring original balance, through path respecting soul individuality and history. Thus, Apometry consolidates as instrument of liberation and awakening, returning to the being possibility of fully inhabiting their own light.

Apometry's fundamental principle resides in controlled dissociation of subtle bodies. Through mental commands and rhythmic counting, usually 1 to 7, the facilitator (known as indoctrinator or conductor) induces conscious unfolding of mediums and assisted. With this, the being's most sensitive parts—like astral body, lower mental body, even causal body—can be isolated, examined, treated directly on spiritual plane, even while physical body remains immobile, in waking state.

When dealing with astral clones, apometric technique offers incomparable resources. First step is spiritual screening. During session, unfolded mediums contact dimensions where clone might be installed. Frequently, these clones are located in dense astral sub-planes, wrapped in containment fields, or coupled to assisted's psychosphere like true parasitic modules. Sometimes, clone isn't immediately visible, requiring meticulous energetic scans, where mediums detect aura distortions, subtle personality duplications, or artificially animated energetic fragments.

Upon locating clone, next step involves containment. Using verbal commands and specific mentalizations, apometrists build magnetic fields or "containment cylinders," isolating clone, preventing reaction or escape. This procedure is essential so clone doesn't automatically return to victim's energy field post-session. At this stage, it's common discovering implants, etheric chips, remote control devices connected to duplicated astral form, all developed by specialized obsessive entities—so-called "shadow scientists."

Next, disconnection is performed. This process consists of cutting fluidic, vibrational links between clone and original person's energy field. Such links usually manifest as cords, energetic tubes, vibrational ties, draining vitality, replicating negative emotional patterns, keeping clone functional. Mediums visualize these cords cut with light swords, symbolic blades, or action of commands like: "We now cut, in name of higher light, all negative, parasitic, manipulative links between original being and its astral clone. May each return to its origin point for treatment or dissolution."

At this point, two possibilities exist. If clone is purely artificial, result of external manipulation without own consciousness spark, it can be immediately dissolved by energetic transmutation. This is done with violet light aid, disintegration commands, or directing form to spiritual transmuting nucleus. However, if clone carries legitimate soul fragments—as in deep trauma cases, repressed subpersonalities, unconscious projections—then process requires delicacy. Clone isn't destroyed, but welcomed, understood, reintegrated into original being. This reintegration is conducted via spiritual indoctrination. Mediums, under spiritual team mentors' guidance, dialogue with clone, identify its beliefs, pains, purposes. Often, these forms think they're protecting original, or live imprisoned in obsolete ideas of guilt, anger, fear. When understood, liberated, these forms gently merge into person's field, re-establishing inner unity. The assisted, in conscious state, might feel intense emotions during this moment: crying, relief, symbolic visions, even vivid recollections of forgotten events. This indicates soul restructuring.

Furthermore, Apometry isn't limited to treating clone. Around this form, obsessors, shadow magicians, karmic pacts, miasmas, thought-forms sustaining or utilizing clone as tool are frequently detected. Session thus transforms into true spiritual sweep, where person's field is cleansed, protected, restored. It's also common for team's spiritual mentors to implant light devices, vibrational shields, energetic reorganizations in chakras and subtle bodies, ensuring newly achieved balance maintains after session ends.

An Apometry differential is technical precision. No improvisation. Serious groups work with well-defined protocols, trained mediumistic teams, opening/closing prayers, detailed reports. Everything documented, discussed, analyzed post-session, ensuring real patient progress tracking. In more severe cases, successive sessions might be scheduled, each focusing on aspect of fragmentation or obsession. This continuity is vital consolidating healing.

Important to note Apometry success depends both on spiritual team action and assisted's disposition. After each session, recommended person maintains elevated spiritual routine: daily prayers, edifying readings, nature contact, light diet, especially emotional vigilance. After all, even after clone removal, internal pattern generating it might try reconstituting if not transformed. Healing is dynamic process, not isolated event.

Apometry, when performed seriously, ethically, with preparation, reveals itself liberating tool. It not only dissolves astral clone but teaches individual they are greater than any fragment, stronger than any shadow, possessing within all keys for reintegration. It is, in essence, path returning to being's center, where no duplicate has space, where original light can finally shine in totality.

Chapter 29
Internal Reintegration

After the elimination of an energetic structure like the astral clone, an internal process begins requiring subtlety, listening, and deep reconnection with one's own essence. The double's absence does not, by itself, mean immediate restoration of internal balance; on the contrary, its removal often reveals psychic gaps, weakened sensory fields, and a transient feeling of emptiness, which can manifest as melancholy, confusion, or disorientation. These manifestations do not indicate regression but signal the energy system is reorganizing after a long period of identity overlap. The space left by the clone needs filling with authentic presence, resuming consciousness in its legitimate centers. This is the moment internal reintegration presents itself not as a choice, but a necessary stage of healing and reconstruction, without which the previously achieved liberation remains incomplete.

Reintegrating internally requires willingness to visit parts of the psyche repressed, ignored, or rejected while the clone acted as a psycho-spiritual substitute. The human being, by abdicating sensitive fragments of their own soul—due to fear, pain, or trauma—opens space for artificial structures forming, which, over time, occupy the true self's place. Removing the clone is, therefore, only the first step. The greater challenge is summoning back these legitimate parts, giving them expression space, allowing them to find their place in the personality's whole. This isn't done hastily or rationalized, but with practices promoting conscious presence, affective listening, openness to what emerges from within.

Reconnecting with these aspects doesn't happen linearly; it's organic, symbolic, profoundly transformative, especially when the individual understands each part of them carries wisdom needing welcome, not combat. It's in this fertile ground of vulnerability that true reconstruction begins. The clone's absence leaves the energy field clearer, but also more exposed, making it essential to strengthen internal structures through constant spiritual practices, authentic emotional expression, physical grounding. Reintegration doesn't just occur on subtle planes; it needs reflection in routine, relationships, how the individual inhabits their own body, positions themselves in the world. This process often involves reviewing habits, breaking old thought patterns, revaluing one's history.

When done with constancy and sensitivity, this return to center results in a more stable vibrational presence, decisions more aligned with the soul, renewed inner strength—not one imposing or controlling, but sustaining, welcoming, guiding consciousness back to its original axis. This phase isn't about exorcising, expelling, cutting—it's about welcoming, embracing, reabsorbing parts of the self dispersed, divided, neglected during the clone's action time. It's a deep, patient healing process, where the person learns to listen to themselves again, observe without judgment, reconstitute their essence's integrity.

The astral clone, most times, doesn't arise from nothing: it's born of pain, trauma, emotional imbalance, repression of important psyche aspects. Therefore, if these aspects don't return to their legitimate center, rupture can repeat. Internal reintegration can happen through various paths, no single formula. One of the most powerful, symbolic is working with deep, conscious visualizations. In relaxed state, eyes closed, rhythmic breathing, person visualizes themselves in safe setting: forest, temple, old house. There, imagines finding "other self"—usually child, adolescent, dark figure, depending on fragment origin. Establishing contact with this lost self part, dialogue begins. Sincere listening is essential: this part has something to say, something forgotten, pain never understood. During visualization, person extends hand, welcomes figure, invites return. When "other self" accepts, both embrace, merge into one body, usually through chest center or third eye. This symbolic image has real impact on subtle planes: represents lost fragment return to consciousness axis. After fusion, practitioner visualizes golden light enveloping entire being, like unity seal. This simple exercise, done sincerely, promotes notable emotional, psychic transformations.

Other reintegration forms involve using words—written or spoken. Writing letters to oneself at different life stages is powerful exercise. Letter written to "wounded self," "self creating clone," or "self manipulated" functions as reconciliation request. Putting on paper feelings never expressed opens space for healing. Practice is even more effective if, after writing, person reads letter aloud to self, before mirror or personal altar, like summoning own soul back to surface.

Psychological therapy is essential ally at this point. Especially approaches dealing with unconscious, like Jungian analytical psychology, past life therapy, family constellation, EMDR, allow buried memories, activated archetypes, ancestral pains integration into conscious safely. In these practices, therapist acts as mirror, guide, helping individual find history's loose ends, stitch with lucidity, compassion, maturity threads.

Spirituality, meanwhile, shouldn't be neglected. Daily meditations, spontaneous prayers, acts of gratitude have irreplaceable role in reintegration. Thanking own body, soul, spirit, for enduring process, is way celebrating unity. Creating small home altar with elements representing restored forces—stones, flowers, personal symbols, protection images—reinforces commitment to new stage. Altar functions as vibrational anchor point, daily reminding fragmentation left behind.

Also important is cultivating grounding, especially after intense disconnection experiences like with active astral clone. Light physical activities like nature walks, touching earth with hands, morning sunbathing, plant care help body remember it's alive, present. Also favor lower chakra alignment, often weakened by long energetic parasitism periods.

Another fundamental aspect is mental pattern vigilance. After clone dissolution, mind might continue operating automatically, repeating ideas, fears, beliefs implanted by duplicate. Necessary identify these remnants, recognize, replace with conscious affirmations. Daily mantras like "I am whole," "My soul is at peace," "I belong to myself," "No part of me is outside me" should be repeated until becoming inner truth. Language has power programming vibrational field, and more this programming conducted with presence, constancy, more it reorders internal system.

It's at this stage true empowerment happens. Person, now freed from clone, begins perceiving how much strength ceded in past—how much possible reconquer. Will returns, eye sparkle reappears, dreams remembered again. Energy field pulses with authenticity. More than that: consciousness expands. What seemed just spiritual problem or emotional disturbance reveals as archetypal journey returning to origin, like hero myth facing shadow, returning transformed.

Internal reintegration is, therefore, great flourishing moment after fragmentation winter. It's when soul sings again with original voice, thoughts align with heart, past ceases being burden, becomes wisdom. Also point where person becomes capable helping others—no longer as victim, but witness of light overcoming illusion mirror. This process doesn't end in day. It's loving, slow, deep reconstruction. But once initiated, path points only one direction: inward. And there, in being's silent core, where no duplicate can reach, resides truth we are whole, always were, always will be.

Chapter 30
Final Care

Ending a cycle of deep spiritual liberation, like removing an astral clone, requires more than simply finalizing energetic procedures—it demands the conscious beginning of a new stage of inner maturity, where self-care assumes a central role. After reintegrating the fragmented essence, the vibrational field enters a delicate stabilization process, where every daily choice directly influences the strengthening or vulnerability of the newly achieved state. It is at this moment that final care ceases being complementary details and becomes structuring foundations of a renewed life. Body, mind, spirit, and emotions need to operate in sync, together sustaining a new level of integrity. This phase represents not the end of a journey, but the beginning of a new cycle of presence, where each conscious gesture collaborates in maintaining the recently conquered freedom.

Living without the clone, although liberating, might initially seem strange to the psyche, accustomed to the repetitive patterns imposed by the energetic duplicate. Therefore, commitment to daily practices of anchoring and purification becomes an indispensable pillar. Each act of self-care—from organizing the environment, natural eating, conscious breathing, to moments of silence, gratitude, prayer—acts as a kind of vibrational reprogramming, signaling to the energy field that the time of fragmentation is past. It's not about obsession with cleansing or spiritual rigidity, but a new ethic of self-care: one understanding spiritual freedom, once achieved, needs cultivation like a rare flower. This cultivation demands attention, but not sacrifice; requires presence, but not perfection. It's a loving process, made of small daily rituals communicating to the soul: "I am here, I am whole, and I choose to remain so."

As this new lifestyle consolidates, the person begins experiencing not just relief from the clone's absence, but the emergence of previously repressed vital force. Creativity returns, senses sharpen, worldview transforms. It's as if the soul, now unobstructed, begins fully occupying internal spaces previously contaminated by alien voices, projected fears, crystallized pains. In this new stage, it becomes evident final care isn't palliative measures, but bridges to life aligned with true self. This life won't be challenge-free, but anchored in lucidity allowing discernment between what's legitimate self part and what's remnant of old plots. Self-care ceases being punctual practice, becomes way of living, where each choice affirms belonging to oneself, each daily gesture, silent prayer of permanence in light.

Final care doesn't refer to grandiose gestures or complicated rituals, but adopting lifestyle prioritizing energetic coherence. First pillar of this care is continuity of spiritual practices. Astral clone, however dissolved, will leave impressions on energy field, like footprints in wet sand. Daily meditations, sincere prayers, using mantras or sacred chants function like tides slowly erasing these traces, re-establishing clean vital energy flow. Mental discipline, in this context, becomes purification tool. Obsessive thoughts, severe self-criticism, constant clone memories should be welcomed with compassion, converted into learning. Each time mind tries returning to drama, gently redirect to present. Conscious breathing techniques, mindfulness, restorative affirmations can be used then. Phrases like "I am at peace with my past," "I am whole now," "Nothing external governs me" reprogram subconscious maintaining new energetic pattern.

Another essential care concerns sleep. During astral clone domination period, many report nocturnal disturbances, nightmares, somnambulism, presence sensation. After liberation, these manifestations might cease spontaneously, but might also persist due to energetic inertia. To ensure restorative, protected sleep, recommended maintain nightly cleansing ritual: light baths with coarse salt, herbs; diffusing essential oils like lavender, cedar; using protection crystals beside bed (like black tourmaline, amethyst); especially, visualizing white light enveloping body before sleep. Simple requests like "May my soul remain protected during sleep" function as commands on subtle plane, shielding natural unfolding occurring during rest hours.

Physical environment lived in must also reflect new vibrational state. Disorganized spaces, with excess objects, mess, dirt, favor dense energy accumulation—same attracting thought-forms, opportunistic entities.

Recommendation is promote physical, energetic environment cleansing, open windows renewing air, use periodic smudging with sage, rosemary, myrrh incense. Also, inherited objects from people with imbalance history, dubious origin gifts, items used during clone influence period can be donated, purified, discarded, as intuition dictates.

Human relationships also deserve attention. During clone action time, common establishing toxic connections—manipulative friendships, dependency-based bonds, family/romantic relations permeated by control, blackmail. After liberation, person sees more clearly who contributes to their light, who insists reactivating old patterns. Breaking toxic ties or establishing new boundaries becomes spiritual protection gesture. No aggression needed—just firmness, clarity, prioritization of own peace.

Physically, body also needs support. Astral clone, while active, compromises vital energy centers like solar plexus, heart, frontal. Therefore, after liberation, natural feeling exhausted, confused, even empty. Response is care for body as if convalescing from long illness. Light diet, constant hydration, outdoor walks, natural therapies (like massage, acupuncture, Reiki), supplements strengthening immune system can accelerate rebalancing process. Avoiding alcohol, processed foods, dense nightlife environments, excessive stimuli recommended until energy field fully restored. Constancy in herb baths can also be maintained few weeks. Mixes with lavender, basil, rosemary, chamomile are gentle, promote balance. If person feels need spiritual reinforcement, can resort to rue, guinea-hen weed bath once week, always finishing with thanksgiving prayers, light visualizations.

Another aspect observed with care is emotional. During clone coexistence, many feelings distorted, blocked, exacerbated. After removal, common old emotions resurface—sadness, anger, fear, guilt. Doesn't mean relapse, but emotional body recalibrating, releasing memories finally healing. Recommendation is welcome feeling without identifying with it. Telling oneself: "This is surfacing for healing" already changes internal posture. If necessary, support therapies like psychotherapy, art therapy, family constellation, regression can aid welcoming these emotional residues.

Fundamental also establish new life purpose. Astral clone, in its action, tends suck not just vital energy, but existential meaning. Many report, while clone active, losing interest in dreams, hobbies, studies, missions. With removal, kind of restart emerges. Sacred opportunity review priorities, rescue old projects, seek new paths. No need change everything at once, but resume small gestures connecting with soul: playing instrument, writing, dancing, praying, walking silently, serving others genuinely.

Avoiding excessive talk about clone or reliving its plot also part final care. Though natural wanting share experience, narrative repetition can keep past energy active. Ideal is transmute experience into learning: keep what useful, release what heavy, move forward. If impulse report, let it be in therapeutic settings or with people prepared listen without judgment, transforming story into useful wisdom.

Most essential care of all: cultivate gratitude. Gratitude for body resisting, soul crying for help, spiritual guides supporting, rituals working, especially for oneself, having courage traverse fragmentation desert finding wholeness. Gratitude is light seal. Each time thanks given, door suffering closes, window healing opens. These final cares aren't mere post-operative. They are, in fact, first steps of new existence—life without clones, projected shadows, but full presence, center, true freedom.

Chapter 31
Complete Liberation

The culmination of a spiritual journey marked by deconstructing illusory patterns, dissolving parasitic entities, and reconnecting with essence is reached when a state of unshakable internal freedom is established with full consciousness. This liberation is not a spectacular event, nor does it depend on external validations or mystical manifestations. It reveals itself, silently, as a whole presence, without noise, shadows, absences. It is the full restoration of the inner axis, when the soul, finally, reassumes command of its energy field without interferences, duplicates, or imposed conditionings. The being, now clean and centered, begins vibrating at their original frequency—the one always existing behind all layers, distortions, fragmentations accumulated by time and pain.

In this state, there's no effort to be who one is; there's only the natural flow of what always was, free from resistances and self-deceptions. With the astral clone's definitive disappearance, the vibrational field reconfigures in harmony with the soul's original matrix, restoring not just psycho-spiritual identity, but also connection with existence's natural cycles. The body becomes more sensitive to life's subtleties, mind gradually silences, feelings assume tone of truth, spontaneity, depth. Absence of internal conflicts allows vital energy circulate fluidly, driving not just healings, but creations. New ideas arise, old dreams resumed, serene enthusiasm for life settles. Intuition sharpens, clearly revealing soul paths. And with it, comes wisdom no longer resisting flow, but dancing with it.

This internal harmony translates into more assertive decisions, more authentic relationships, presence posture radiating peace even amidst external chaos. What establishes, finally, is new self-awareness: expanded perception understanding depth of own crossing, recognizing, with humility, lucidity, pain's role as awakening instrument. Clone, however dysfunctional, served as mirror revealing what needed looking at, welcoming, healing. Overcoming it is, ultimately, transcending old pacts with fear, guilt, self-forgetting. And, reaching this clarity, sovereignty point, being doesn't return to what was before—they are born to new version of self, more integrated, lucid, free.

True liberation isn't just end of invisible prison; it's beginning of life where every gesture, word, thought aligned with being's truth. It's soul maturity assuming place in world—without noise, veils, with silent firmness of one finally returned home.

This liberation isn't just clone absence. It is, above all, full self presence. State where individual no longer divides between conflicting internal forces, dissonant voices, contradictory impulses. Vital energy flows again without deviation, like river finding original bed after years dammed by invisible obstacle. And when this energy re-establishes, everything flourishes: mental clarity, physical vigor, emotional stability, especially, spiritual sovereignty.

At this journey point, common individual experiences series unusual sensations. One is lightness. As if body, inside, emptied of old, ancestral weight. Shoulders relax, heart quiets, breathing becomes ample. Sleeping ceases being escape, becomes rest. Waking ceases being battle, transforms into reunion. Rhythm re-establishes, as if life danced again in right tempo.

Another complete liberation sign is genuine identity return. Person starts remembering who they were before interferences. Resumes forgotten tastes, neglected skills, old desires seeming erased. More than that: starts discovering new self aspects, talents dormant under duplicate energy weight. As if, eliminating clone, space occupied by it filled by new creative spark, now aligned with true essence.

Intuition also expands. Without clone's vibrational noise acting as dissonant antenna, person starts hearing inner voice more clearly. Decisions become easier, signs clearer, synchronicities more frequent. As if universe responds again in real time, paths open fluidly, no internal blocks boycotting soul's legitimate desires.

But perhaps liberation's deepest aspect is empowerment. Perception that, however much external help—mediums, shamans, therapists, mentors—it was own soul choosing liberation. Own consciousness saying: enough. This recognition is transformative. Person stops seeing self as invisible forces victim, starts understanding self co-creator of reality. This posture change is true antidote against future clone formations or other energetic parasitism forms.

Complete liberation also brings mission sense. One doesn't pass unscathed through such experience. Surviving astral clone is traversing own intimate hell, looking in mirror, facing not just what created by external forces, but also what fed internally. This dive brings maturity, discernment, compassion. And many reaching this point feel almost natural call help others. Not as saviors, but living witnesses liberation is possible. That light is real. That soul can reintegrate. Some choose study deeper spiritual universe, diving into esoteric schools, energy healing lines, ancestral practices. Others become therapists, mentors, silent examples. Path doesn't matter. What matters is lucidity seed planted consciousness center: once liberated, being starts radiating cohesion field so potent its simple presence destabilizes dissonant energies around. Becomes vibrational order focus in often chaotic world.

But liberation also brings responsibilities. Main one is staying centered. Clone, even dissolved, might try reinstalling through old patterns, especially if vigilance decreases. Not by own strength, as it no longer exists, but psyche's natural tendency recreating comfort zones, even if harmful. Therefore, maintaining healthy habits, energetic cleansing routines, self-knowledge practices isn't optional—it's part new life.

Another responsibility is with truth. Liberated being needs honesty with self, abandon masks, assume light, shadow humbly. Pretending be who not, or trying please external standards detriment own essence, are open doors new fragmentations. Integrity, at this stage, isn't moralism—it's energetic survival.

Life, after complete liberation, gains another texture. Small pleasures become intense: water taste, sun warmth, animal silent presence, sincere hug from someone seeing soul beyond appearance. Everything seems more real, no filters interfering perception. As if veil lifted, person, finally, living inside out, harmony with central axis.

Many, reaching this point, ask: why did I need go through all this? Though no single answer, common feeling: necessary. Clone, however terrible, served catalyst much deeper process—awakening process. Without it, perhaps soul remained dormant, dispersed, divided between roles, obligations not dialoguing with inner truth. Clone was distorted mirror forcing being seek original image. This perception doesn't justify suffering, but reframes it. Pain becomes master. Fear becomes compass. Loss becomes portal. And, in end, what seemed nightmare reveals rite of passage: from false self to true self. Fragmentation to wholeness. Survival to full life.

Complete liberation is, thus, apex of journey often initiated without consciousness. Journey passing through dense shadows, emotional labyrinths, invisible combats, sleepless nights, silent tears. But ending—or perhaps beginning—with luminous certainty: soul returned home. And inside this house, now clean, whole, silent, it can, finally, rest... and live.

Epilogue

Throughout these pages, you have traversed invisible paths, delved into the multiple layers of being, and, perhaps for the first time, clearly saw reflected the face of your shadow: the astral clone. This reflection, often ignored or feared, was exposed here with honesty, depth, and courage. You understood it can be born from repressed traumas, intensely sustained emotions, poorly conducted spiritual practices—and, yes, can also be architected by external forces with hidden intentions. But more important than knowing *how* it is born, is understanding *why* it remains. The astral clone exists as long as imbalance exists. It is the internal universe's answer to an unasked question. It is the echo of an unheard cry. It is the living symbol of parts of you left behind.

Now, reaching the end of this reading, a new stage begins: that of reintegration. It's not about eliminating or destroying. The highest path is not violence against oneself, but loving lucidity. Dissolving the astral clone is not a battle—it's healing. It's the moment you recognize the origin of what seemed an enemy, see in it a fragment of your own being, trying to survive on the margin of your consciousness.

You learned everything vibrates. Everything molds. And everything created on the astral plane can be transformed. The clone is not immutable. It responds to your choices, attention, awakened gaze. And the more you know yourself, the less it needs to exist.

But this journey doesn't end here. This epilogue isn't a final point—it's an opening. Because, now possessing knowledge, responsibility is yours. No longer live automatically. No longer give your energy repeating old pains. No longer allow external forces manipulate soul fragments without permission. Consciousness is your sword and cure. Knowledge, luminous armor. Spiritual practice, path reintegrating what dissociated.

You also discovered astral clone existence is call—reminder parts of you forgotten, wounded, dormant. And each asks attention, not dominate, but heal. Recognizing these parts, you don't weaken—you become whole.

And this wholeness changes everything. Changes how you think, feel, relate. Changes energetic patterns you emit. Changes quality of presence in world. Because integrated being isn't dominated by fear, guilt, self-judgment. Guided by clarity, intuition, deep self-love.

If something in you stirred during this reading—recognized symptoms, felt unease, accessed forgotten memories—know: you already initiated dissolution process. Because *seeing* clone is first step deactivating its power. Those living under unconscious astral duplicates influence often have no idea they carry vibrational distortion field within. Act, feel, decide under silent command fragmented part. But you are no longer one of them. You saw. You knew. You freed yourself.

And now? Now is time practice. Maintain internal vigilance. Cultivate pure emotions. Choose thoughts aligned with who you truly desire be. Filter wisely what enters mind, exits mouth, pulses from heart.

You are center your energy field. No entity more powerful in life than own awakened consciousness. Neither obsessors, negative magicians, collective egregores have greater strength than being knowing, loving self entirely. And when this happens, astral clone—finding no vibrational sustenance—begins weakening. Returns source. Dissolves ether. What was shadow becomes strength. Pain becomes wisdom. Fragment becomes integrated light.

At this point, you not only heal—you transform into healing channel for world. Because who reintegrates, radiates. Who recognizes, inspires. Who liberates, awakens others. Therefore, this book doesn't end in you. Continues in gazes you'll meet, conversations you'll have, choices you'll make. Your presence will change. Field vibrate differently. World, even subtly, transform with you.

Hidden mirror journey is, ultimately, journey returning inner home. And now, closing these pages, you know: true home never outside. Always there—in silent center your consciousness.

Welcome back.

www.ingramcontent.com/pod-product-compliance
Lightning Source LLC
LaVergne TN
LVHW040051080526
838202LV00045B/3582